MARGARET MCCURRY

CONSTRUCTING TWENTY-FIVE SHORT ST

Wilmette Public Library
Wilmette, Illinois
Telephone: 256-5025

GAYLORD M

MARGARET McCURRY

CONSTRUCTING TWENTY-FIVE SHORT STORIES

THE MONACELLI PRESS

First published in the United States of
America in 2000 by
The Monacelli Press, Inc.
10 East 92nd Street
New York, New York 10128.

Copyright © 2000
The Monacelli Press, Inc.

Library of Congress
Cataloging-in-Publication Data
McCurry, Margaret.
Margaret McCurry : constructing
twenty-five short stories.
p.   cm.
Includes bibliographical references.
ISBN 1-58093-046-8
1. McCurry, Margaret. 2. Architects—
United States—Biography. 3. Architecture,
Modern—20th century—United States.
I. Title: Constructing twenty-five short
stories. II. Title: Constructing 25 short
stories. III. Title.
NA737.M436   A2   2000
720'.92—dc21   99-53960

Printed in China

Designed by Abigail Sturges

CONTENTS

INSIDE OUT

On Becoming an Architect

This is the story of one architect's attempt to be heard in a world where the art of architecture has a diminishing voice in the shaping of cities and making of places. My voice in this book is tuned to a world where the stepping stones to positions of influence over the built environment must be laid by hand, one by one.

To build well and meaningfully is the challenge that confronts every architect. Whether choosing to distill or redefine historically identifiable forms or to create new forms altogether, one is faced with the question of how to practice an architecture defined by Random House as "the profession of designing . . . artificial constructions and environments, usually with some regard to aesthetic effect." How often in this profession is the architect praised as having "good hands," "a good eye," or "a good mind"? How are these physical entities transformed into the finely tuned instruments necessary for creating an architecture of substance? How does one develop the sensibility needed to elevate the enclosing of space or the molding of form into an aesthetic act relevant to its specific time and place? And how does one create an architecture that fulfills the mandate of Luis Barragán, who once stated that "any work of architecture that does not express serenity is a mistake"? For the past thirty years, I have pursued this achievement of "aesthetic effect" and this search for an architecture that attains a harmonious and tranquil relationship to the world.

The development of my own hands and eyes was a slow evolution. My hands were trained first to become those of an artist. From early childhood, I was both inclined and encouraged to draw and paint. My eye was also made more acute in its vision by eleven years of apprenticeship at the Chicago office of Skidmore, Owings & Merrill (SOM). There, beginning in 1966, I learned the basics of the Miesian aesthetic as practiced by the master's disciples, many of whom had joined SOM after apprenticing in Ludwig Mies van der Rohe's office, or directly upon graduation from the Illinois Institute of Technology, where Mies was the director from 1937 until he was fired in 1959. The architectural maturation of my mind really began

when I was reintroduced to my future husband, Stanley Tigerman, on a late summer day in 1975. Some years earlier on another summer evening my father, Paul D. McCurry, a fellow architect, had introduced me to Stanley at an official American Institute of Architects (AIA) outing in one of the city's parks. Dressed for the occasion in a straw boater, bow tie, and white bucks, Stanley was suitably impressive, as might befit one of the young turks of the Chicago architectural community. He made short shrift of his conversation with an unknown on the scene. I was reminded of the snub from time to time over the ensuing years because we resided in adjacent Mies van der Rohe apartment buildings and I would occasionally glimpse his monochromatically clad figure hailing taxis or hauling groceries. When he unexpectedly called on an August evening years later I accepted his invitation for an introductory drink, anticipating an opportunity for redress. Until that day in 1975, I had lead an intellectually doctrinaire and rather insular life at SOM.

The eye that I acquired at the firm was one for detail and proportion; I also gained an understanding of the scale and use of materials within the modernist tradition. My education went so far into detailing refinement that I learned the crucial difference between a ⅛-inch reveal and a ⅜-inch one, but it fell short of imparting an intellectual rationale for design. By the time I worked at SOM, the firm was firmly entrenched in reinterpretations of Mies within the framework of the module and in attempting to adhere to Sullivan's dictate that "form follows function." There was a right way and a wrong way to do just about everything. Such practice at its best produced a body of artisans skilled in technological invention who branched out into other firms, spreading the system. At its worst, SOM discouraged intellectual invention, the ethic being one of "build, don't talk." Stanley Tigerman had worked there in the late 1950s, prior to his departure for Yale. He thus understood but was discouraged by my lack of knowledge of the work of his friends, the preeminent new stars in the architectural firmament who had categorized themselves on the East Coast as the Whites, descendants of Le Corbusier whose formalist tabula rasa excluded history, and the Grays, who were the inclusive functionalists; and on the West Coast as the Silvers, who were extruders of metal-curtain-wall high-rises, to say nothing of the Chicago Seven, a hybrid group he was just forming. He provided me with copies of all his published work and that of his friends as well. I had entered SOM almost directly from Vassar and was fully prepared to embrace the principles of modernism as doctrine.

My work has gradually evolved into a synthesis of modern classicism and the eccentric romanticism often found in the naive architecture of the American vernacular. By clarifying and contemporizing classical forms, traditional icons become new while still evoking familiar memories and associations. Relying upon order and symmetry, I seek to compose places that achieve calm and comfort; their siting is harmonious with nature but they remain sentinels separated from

it. I have been concerned with processes of refinement and distillation, the paring away of the unessential to locate the essence. What is straightforward and elemental is universally understood; direct expression defies sentimentality.

In late September 1942, nine months after Pearl Harbor, I was born in Chicago. My artistic parents named me Margaret, after Mars, the Roman god of war, modified by the middle name of Irene (my mother's name), the Greek goddess of peace. My birth was announced on a card designed by my architect father and printed on blueprint paper. I was brought home to live at 9350 South Hamilton Avenue, Beverly Hills, a neighborhood of Chicago's far South Side, in an International Style house designed in 1936 by my father. Two years later, my sister, Marian (also a derivative of Mars), was born, and in 1946 my brother, Alan, completed the family circle.

My father had been classically trained in the beaux-arts tradition in the 1920s at the Armour Institute (today the Illinois Institute of Technology) and the Art Institute of Chicago. Despite this, he impatiently tracked contemporary movements surfacing in Europe. A poor boy from Engelwood, an Irish neighborhood on the South Side of the city, he worked summers detailing neo-Gothic churches and gravestones for his teacher, Thomas Tallmadge, of Tallmadge & Watson (a descendant of D. H. Burnham and Company), until he had saved enough money to take himself on the grand tour in 1928–29, in pursuit of the new architecture. Along the way he accumulated enough stories of his adventures to enliven the dinner table for the next half century. My father returned from abroad a confirmed modernist. It was the beginning of the Great Depression. As architecture slowed to a standstill, he worked for the feisty art deco architect Andrew

Rebori, who was also a critic at the Chicago Architectural Sketch Club, of which they were both members. As the Depression deepened, Rebori's work dried up, and my father joined friends in D. H. Burnham and Company to work on Chicago's 1933 Century of Progress Exposition, which was designed by Joseph Urban. This was the second World's Fair held in Chicago. The first was the famed World's Columbian Exposition forty years earlier, in 1893. The site was along the lakefront to the south of the city, starting at the Adler Planetarium and encompassing two lagoons as it spread south paralleling the Illinois Central Railroad. My father was eventually dislodged by Hubert Burnham, Daniel's nephew, and replaced by Nathaniel Owings and his brother-in-law, Louis Skidmore, who subsequently formed SOM. His search for work led to a two-year stint in the state architect's office in Springfield, where he rebuilt the dome of the capitol and restored the village of New Salem, Abraham Lincoln's early home.

My father spent time during the summer in Saugatuck, Michigan, at Oxbow, the summer school of the Art Institute of Chicago. There, on the sandy shores of Lake Michigan, many out-of-work architects and artists gathered to paint and teach. There he met and in 1935 married my mother, Irene Bell Tipler, a fellow South Sider. My mother had just returned from New York after completing a master's program at Columbia Teachers College and was hired to teach art in Chicago's public schools. As state appropriations for restorations ran out, my father also acquired his master's degree in teaching and became a drafting and mathematics teacher at Lane Technical High School. Thus began a ten-year stint in education for the two of them. My mother became chairman of the art department at Harper High School and later illustrated books for the Board of Education, a position she would relinquish to my father when I was born. With the assistance of two salaries, an occasional architectural commission, and a contribution from my maternal grandfather (a prominent dentist who had moved to Beverly Hills in the early 1920s), the optimistic young couple—who had eloped to Europe, toured the Netherlands, tied the knot in London, and retreated from the rising Third Reich in Germany—returned home to defy the Depression and build their 1,700-square-foot dream house on a 50-foot-wide piece of Illinois prairie in the same South Side community.

Wedged between a red-brick Georgian on the north and a brown-brick Tudor on the south, their modern white-brick house sported the requisite silica-brick black base and glass-block inserts. With my father's shingle prominently planted on the front lawn, the house was published in the January 1938 issue of *American Home Magazine*. Thumbing through the oft-read, ten-cent copy, I can recall memories of life in the only "modern" house around. In those pre-air-conditioned times I especially remember the sweltering summers. Too far inland from the lake to bene-

fit from its cooling breezes, we sometimes slept out-of-doors on the sleeping porch that overlooked the rear garden. My sister and I shared the bedroom whose corner window opened onto this porch. Its only drawback was drainage: the run-off from summer storms that blew up quickly in the night would cause a back flow, and the cry to bail would go out. Rousted from our beds and standing ankle-deep in water, the whole family worked the bucket brigade to prevent the water from rising over the sill and flooding the adjoining master bedroom. Clearly this was the most dramatic effect of the modernist movement that had dictated the flat roofline, but the most meaningful one was the quality of afternoon light that poured through the glass-block walls and steel windows and doors on the rear facade. The house's open plan permitted this western light to penetrate the whole interior, warming us in the winter and beckoning us out to play on the lawn in the summer. The windowless side facades brought privacy and, in turn, protected the neighbors from our vociferous play. A sense of restful security permeated the house, and the flowing lines of the art deco furnishings reinforced these feelings. On top of the white enameled bedsteads that bracketed the white headboard in my parent's room reposed a prized pair of lamps that were designed by George Fred Keck, the architect of the "House of Tomorrow" at the 1933 Century of Progress Exposition. These stately bronze stemmed lamps, with their conical milk-glass shades, cast a soft light over our reading of the Golden Books. My paternal grandmother, Ella Crissinger McCurry—who as a young girl had crossed the West by train and then by stage to teach in a one-room schoolhouse in rural Oregon—shared the bedroom over the garage with her Danish nurse and our au pair, "Nursey." Crippled by a stroke and confined to a wheelchair, my

grandmother taught me to read before I entered the first grade.

While I was growing up, my father was benefiting from the revival of the profession of architecture after the war. He had stopped work at the Board of Education and joined his friends Vale Faro and Al Bacci at Schmidt, Garden & Erickson, the venerable firm that under Hugh Garden's leadership had designed the first reinforced-concrete building in Chicago—the Montgomery Ward warehouse. My father soon became a partner specializing in schools and hospitals and began to speak out for the profession. Eventually, as president of the Chicago chapter of the American Institute of Architects in 1966–67, he would earn his Fellowship by leading the movement to defeat the elevated crosstown expressway. This had been proposed by the city's engineers and supported by the firm I had just entered, SOM, and it would have destroyed many historic neighbor-

hoods. He went on to present Mies van der Rohe with the gold medal of the chapter during his presidency and sponsored Stanley for Fellowship in 1972. My father would live just long enough to learn that I was admitted to the College of Fellows in the spring of 1991 and that the induction would occur during the AIA convention in Washington, D.C., where he had received his own medal some twenty-five years before.

Several of my father's watercolors hung on the walls of our family's house, alongside the still lifes that my mother painted. Our own youthful experiments with paint were relegated to the basement. Sketching was especially encouraged. My early drawings were primarily of horses—pintos, piebalds, and especially palominos, since my imaginary childhood companion was Roy Rogers's horse, Trigger. Together we would canter about the neighborhood, stopping at houses under construction, where I hitched him to any convenient post while I climbed throughout the structure, using the roof beam as a tightrope and the joists as stationary trapezes. I collected as play money the plugs from electrical junction boxes, and I built sand castles in the piles of mortar mix. At an early age I began going along with my father to school construction sites. Later, my younger sister Marian and, later still, my brother Alan joined the entourage. I remember the sets of blueprints stacked on makeshift wooden desks in dusty trailers and my father and the contractor paging through them while I snooped around. The sights and sounds of construction filled my senses—the smell of fresh lumber wafting through the trailer window, the rhythmic sound of hammers pounding nails, the awesome sight of structures being assembled before my eyes. These site inspections were the high point of my exposure to the building process.

On many evenings, my father and I built structures with the Erector Set on the dining-room table, and I constructed ranch buildings with my Lincoln Log kit to house my toy horse collection. When I wasn't playing indoors, I was out and about catching butterflies in nets along the railroad right-of-way, capturing garter snakes among the tall prairie grasses, and making a bow and arrow out of the neighbor's bushes. One year I planted and tended a small garden behind the garage, harvesting my first crop of a dozen ears of corn, contorted carrots, and warped cucumbers. My family followed the same pursuits as many middle-class Chicago families: the yearly spring visit to the Shriner's Circus at the Media Temple signaled the start of the entertainment season, which ended on Labor Day at the River View Ramble in the amusement park, home to the infamous "Bobs" roller coaster. The sounds associated with summer on Hamilton Avenue were those of the gong on the knife-grinder's cart as he plied the back alleyway by day, and of the bells mounted on the Good Humor truck that canvassed the street at dusk. In winter snow fell softly, piling up on the toboggan run in the forest preserve at Eighty-seventh Street, where we also learned to skate on the flooded baseball diamond and form snow angels in the outfield. Into that seemingly ideal world fell my first experience with a discrimination that was to continue throughout my working years (and of course, those of many other working women). It occurred the fall I entered the fifth grade wearing, as usual, my corduroy overalls. After that first day of class, a note from the principal advised my parents that little girls were to attend class in dresses. From then on, from running races and sliding into bases, my knees and shins were always skinned.

So it was not a perfect world, and discrimination occurred at many levels. Beverly Hills at that time was a segregated community tucked into the city's far southwest corner. Its mile-wide limits were Ashland Avenue on the east and Western Avenue on the west, and my parents set those streets as my own boundaries. I chafed at the rules that curtailed my exploration of new neighborhoods and secretly pushed beyond them on my Schwinn New World bicycle.

Every Saturday morning in the summer, from the age of ten, I had ridden the Rock Island Railroad into the city with my friend Sandy Schlentz to attend drawing classes at the School of the Art Institute. Beginning at Forty-seventh Street, the raised roadbed bisected Bronzeville, a historic African-American neighborhood that was a vibrant and self-sufficient community between the wars. By the time I passed through, the housing stock had deteriorated, but I saw memorable vignettes of family life unfolding on the back porches and through the open windows of the tenements that flashed past as I pressed my face against dirty glass. That immediacy left an indelible impression of an intense urban density.

Fifteen years later, as an adult, I was to pass through Bronzeville as a member of the Chicago Beautiful Committee, an organization formed by Sis Daley, the mayor's wife, to search out and reward individuals or communities that had improved and beautified their property. The tenements I remembered from my childhood were gone. The area was now bracketed by the Dan Ryan Expressway and the Robert Taylor Homes, those mega-block modern apartment complexes so favored by urban renewalists. The low neighborhoods had vanished, and there were certainly no candidates for beautification awards in the grassless expanses between the high-rises.

I was to be reminded of the lost neighborhood for many more years as Stanley and I drove past those projects on the Dan Ryan, our route around the bottom of the lake to our weekend home in Michigan on the opposite shore. Recently I found an opportunity to become involved with the Bronzeville community. In 1994, as a member of the Alumni/ae Council of the Graduate School of Design at Harvard University (I was a Loeb Fellow at the GSD in 1986–87), I learned that there were urban design studios that tackled tough planning issues posed by actual clients who funded the studios. Most of the sponsors were foreign governments or corporations, but I felt that the energies of these graduate students should be directed toward finding solutions to urban issues in Chicago. It took two years and a joint venture with the Illinois Institute of Technology, whose campus abuts Thirty-fifth Street and the Bronzeville neighborhood, to persuade the powers that be that this student consortium could produce some positive planning ideas. A friend and client whose husband had graduated from the Harvard Business School donated the funding in his memory and the study of the Thirty-fifth Street corridor, from its western terminus at Comiskey Park (the new White Sox ballpark) to its eastern end at Martin Luther King Drive, had begun. A semester later, three plans for the redevelopment of Thirty-fifth Street were coalesced into a report entitled "A Street in Bronzeville." Students and residents worked together to produce the material for this revitalization study, which has been disseminated throughout Chicago and other cities. Restoration has already begun on historic landmarks such as the Chicago Bee Building, the handsome terra-cotta faced art deco building designed for this influential Sunday newspaper in the early 1930s.

On a midsummer weekend our family traveled to Elkhart, Indiana, for the McCurry/Crissinger reunion. The route took us south and then east around the bottom of the lake on the old Route 41, which skirted the steel mills of Gary, Indiana. Black smoke belched from their blast furnaces, and orange flames shot up from tall brick chimneys. Seen from below, their rusting steel structures towered over us as our old Ford Zephyr

coughed and wheezed its way past them. Today, on the weekends that Stanley and I drive to our cottage in Michigan, we pass these same moldering complexes. Seen now at eye level from the elevated Skyway, their power has not diminished with age, and their industrial forms still reoccur in our work.

Every August the family climbed into our current blue Ford motorcar to begin summer vacation, always an exploration of architecture and history. Eventually we crisscrossed the nation from coast to coast, in and out of every major city and its suburbs, along every walking tour and into every museum. We hiked across Civil War battlefields in the East and hunted for Indian arrowheads and gold nuggets in the West. The only time we ever paused in this frenzied marathon was the week we spent in Aspen, Colorado, when I was eight, but even then horseback rides during the day were traded for evenings in the music tent. Some in the family attribute my almost maniacal ability for the maximum arrangement of rooms in the minimum square footage to my role as a trunk packer on these excursions.

The places that we saw during those years that I remember most vividly were those where we came

closely into contact with the land and the remains or reenactments of civilizations. The stark ruins of the Anasazi's stone cliff dwellings at Mesa Verde in the Four Corners region became as strong a reminder of the constructs of a civilization as the tidy masonry-and-wood build-

ings of colonial Williamsburg, laid out in orderly grids along the dirt streets of this Tidewater community, which was so influential in the formation of a national aesthetic.

A favorite local excursion was the drive to downtown Chicago. We always drove into the Loop from the southwest by way of the boulevards of the Burnham plan, or directly from the south along Lake Shore Drive through Frederick Law Olmsted's Jackson Park. As we rounded the last curve and the drive straightened along the shore to run parallel to Michigan Avenue through Grant Park and past Buckingham Fountain, the great wall of the city aligned itself with this axis. Only the Art Institute planted itself on the eastern side of the avenue, its blocky limestone form interrupting the tranquillity of the park. Directly across the avenue, on top of the Orchestra Hall building, perched the Cliff Dwellers Club.

Founded in 1907 as the Attic Club by the Midwestern writer Hamlin Garland, his brother-in-law Lorado Taft (a sculptor), and assorted architects who had assembled in Chicago to participate in the 1893 World's Fair, the club was incorporated as the Cliff Dwellers two years later. Member Daniel H. Burnham was hired to create a penthouse atop his existing Orchestra Hall building. Howard van Doren Shaw, another member, was recruited to design the interior. With a benediction from President Teddy Roosevelt, the kiva fire was lit in 1909. The charter called for it to be a "rallying point for the Midland Arts," and it did indeed become home to many members of the Chicago Sketch Club. Even Louis Sullivan joined in 1912. In his last unhappy, largely forgotten years, when he was eking out a living in a shabby hotel on the South Side of the city, Sullivan was supported by certain club members who commissioned him to design twenty plates to illustrate his philosophy of ornament. This he did sitting at a loaner desk in the headquarters of the terra-cotta company that had produced many of his designs in his heyday years before. His Cliff Dweller friends also arranged for him to write his autobiography, for which he was paid one hundred dollars a month. His memoirs were written in the library of the club after a series of dinners paid for by the members, and it was here that my father, then a student at the Armour Institute, was brought by his professors to sit and listen to Sullivan's stories. So it was little wonder that some years later, as a young professional, my father joined his compatriots in climbing the thirty-one worn marble stairs that ascended to this special aerie. With the offices of Schmidt, Garden & Erickson located atop an adjacent "skyscraper," he lunched there every day, most often at the Club Table where an assortment of artists, writers, and architects dined under the watchful eye of a gigantic stuffed gaur head shot by one of the lay members on safari at the turn of the century. This trophy hung above a Stickley sideboard, upon which reposed a great Jarvie hammered-silver punch bowl. Oak-paneled and wainscoted walls formed three sides of this great vaulted hall, which measured seventy by twenty-eight feet. The fourth side was rhythmically punctuated by tall french doors that opened to the east onto a balconied terrace, which overlooked Michigan Avenue, Grant Park, and the Monroe Street Harbor.

In the summer, on our Saturday sojourns to the city, we were often joined while dining on the terrace by my father's colleagues. There the talk was most always of architecture. My father also occasionally brought us to the club in the evenings when guests were invited for special programs. Much was made of us as we dutifully sat through musicales and lectures. It was a magical place of camaraderie—its paneled walls hung with members' art, its shelves filled with books written by or about club members, its scarred leather club chairs grouped about the limestone fireplace, its soft-spoken and congenial staff. As a child I never doubted that I, too, would become a member of this special community when I grew up. Never seeing it segregated by gender at lunch, it had not occurred to me that this was a place that would, in time, open wide its doors to my brother and brother-in-law but keep them tightly closed to my sister and myself.

As a young architect I debated this policy with my father, positing the position that only professional women should be admitted, like their male counterparts, and that if spouses of either gender desired entry they could choose to apply for separate lay memberships. Change was slow to come, and gradually some of the club's most promising younger members resigned in protest. During these years I rarely visited the club. But at Christmas in 1978, I had agreed to marry Stanley on March 17 of the following year. We hoped to hold the wedding reception at the Arts Club of Chicago, where we were members, with its elegant Mies van der Rohe interior, but the Saturday date was booked. Rather than relinquish Saint Patrick's Day (an occasion selected by Stanley in celebration of my Irish heritage), we reluctantly acceded to my father's wishes and signed up the Cliff Dwellers.

When the flood gates to the Cliff Dwellers were finally opened in 1984, I received a call inviting me to become one of the first women members. But the call had come too late, and I regretfully declined.

When I was twelve, my father and mother moved us from our urban enclave to the greener educational pastures of the northern suburbs. Suburbia was a major readjustment for me. The "city" of Lake Forest was a three-mile bicycle ride from the Campbell subdivision and the partially completed spec home into which my father deposited us on a June day in 1955. The fact that he had designed this white-brick ranch house for his friend the developer Marshall Campbell was a small consolation. Fully intending to build dream house number two someday, he nevertheless landscaped this "temporary" corner acre by calling upon the considerable talents of his good friend Franz Lipp, the renowned Austrian landscape architect who planted so many varieties of trees on our property that I completely filled my high-school botany-class notebook with specimens from our land.

I did eventually adjust to country life, as a child will, especially as I discovered that the work of such seminal architects as Howard van Doren Shaw and David Adler abounded in our community. Market Square, designed by Shaw in 1916 as an English village, is undoubtedly one of the most elegantly proportioned shopping areas in the country. Surrounded by shops on three sides, with a fountain at its entrance, the square steps outward from a central park toward the one-way street with angled parking that wraps around it to another shady parkway buffering the sidewalk and shop windows. The first watercolor I painted in my new environment was of this sunlit square. My mother and I were to paint many more watercolors during those years. She had been trained by Charles Martin at Columbia Teachers College and spent one summer in Provincetown painting. We had several teachers from Lake Forest College for our Saturday classes, one of them being Franz Schulze, author of a biography of Philip Johnson. My best watercolors were of David Adler's works—Shore Acres and the Blair and Hamill houses and his own French Normandy farmhouse in Libertyville. Once a year, on the Lake Forest House and Garden Walk, many of his homes were open, along with those of Shaw and of Harrie T. Lindeberg. My brother attended secondary school at Lake Forest Academy, the former Mellody Farm that was housed in Arthur Huen's Italian Renaissance villa, originally designed for J. Odgen Armour of the Armour Meat Packing family, in West Lake Forest. New ownership and security concerns canceled all public excursions years ago, but my memory of these extraordinary houses remains intact. This new world I had come to was originally the summer playground for Chicago's rich and famous, whose majestic estates dotted the countryside and lined the bluffs above Lake Michigan along Lake Road. Needless to say, our small subdivision was one of the results of the breakup of these large properties, which began during the Great Depression. When we first moved into the community, father discovered that the waiting list at the Lindeberg-designed Onwentsia Country Club was ten years. Since that time span did not suit him, he organized a group of newcomers and founded the Lake Forest Club. He contributed his designs for the clubhouse and pool, so even our leisure time was spent in a McCurry creation.

Most of the old families sent their children to private schools, so Lake Forest High School was populated by assorted newcomers and the descendants of workers employed on the estates. It prepared me well for my later higher education. In August of my junior year, the family dedicated its summer vacation to the systematic study of the Eastern colleges and specifically the Seven Sisters, as certain women's colleges were known. After two weeks of a whirlwind series of tours and interviews, all seven began to blur. But I had retained a strong memory of Vassar College's massive stone gateway, above which reposed the art-history department. I filled out an early-decision application to the school, and when I was accepted in December, I agreed to join Vassar's one-hundredth class.

The four years I spent at Vassar focused less on architecture (although as an art-history major I took what courses the school offered in that subject) and more on intense study interspersed with intense play. I was an English minor and spent many hours studying European and American literature. Reading the words of distinguished novelists, playwrights, and poets, I fell under the spell of language: "And the thoughts of youth are long, long thoughts." This refrain from Longfellow's poem "My Lost Youth" seems to personify those college years.

What architecture I did absorb that did not come from books came from what was extant on my own campus or on the many campuses of the men's colleges that my classmates and I visited over various weekends. I

remember being told by an architecture student at Yale that Eero Saarinen's Stiles and Morse Colleges were influenced by the Italian hill town of San Gimignano, and since I too lived in a Saarinen dorm, Noyes, that comparison lingered in my memory until I could confirm it twenty years later. What I do still remember about my years in Noyes was that all the furniture was built in and the ceilings seemed low in comparison to those of its Gothic neighbors.

Carrying six courses a semester, I managed to obtain a humanist education while simultaneously earning credits sketching and painting from the model and studying mechanical drawing and design. The portfolio of drawings that I amassed in four years eventually led to my acceptance as a member of the interior-design department in the Chicago office of SOM two years after graduation. But first I had to experience the realities of the 1964 workplace for a young woman with a bachelor of arts degree. What I received from Vassar besides a fine education is what the Seven Sisters were famous for imparting, a strong sense of self-worth and the ability to confront life's circumstances with confidence in one's capabilities. But in spite of my college degree, it was a well-known fact in those days that, for a woman, the only way into any company was through the secretarial door. My parents, of course, had pushed for a continuation of my education. In fact, every summer I was in college, I was sent to summer school to pick up those necessary but singularly uninspiring education courses that were required for a teaching certificate. Yet in the end I preferred to search for a job elsewhere, preferably, but not necessarily, related to the arts.

That first summer after graduation, I found myself signed up for a speedwriting and typing course taught by a retired secretary. In that same class on the North Shore was another friend from Vassar and several other representatives from the Seven Sisters. While I was pounding on my typewriter staccato style in secretarial class, my sister and brother were enrolled by my father in an architectural class taught by Stanley Tigerman at the University of Illinois and open to students of all persuasions. The two would come home at night and recount stories of an eccentric teacher who extolled them on to design excellence while gnawing on a white handkerchief. At the end of a summer of making models of housing projects, Alan remained an English major, eventually entering the library sciences, but Marian returned to Vassar and changed her major from pre-med to art history and subsequently attended architecture school. Enrolled in that same historic class of Stanley's was my future brother-in-law, Douglas Tweedie. Today, Marian and Douglas are both in the profession. Meanwhile, graduating from secretarial school, I selected from the roster of an employment agency a job interview for a position as secretary to the head of the package-design department at Quaker Oats, and got the job.

How to convince people to purchase products based on the design of a box or can wrapper was an interesting phenomenon that seemed to engage a number of fascinating people in the advertising profession. And so six months after I began, when the position of package-design coordinator became available, I lobbied for the job. The next year I shuttled back and forth to New York, reviewing packaging comps with famous ad agencies such as Lee Vitale and supervising product photography. A perfectionist, I once cooked the pancakes for the Aunt Jemima Buttermilk Pancake wrapper because the stylist assigned to prepare them could not make their tops sufficiently lacy. I was one of only five women above the level of secretary in all of Quaker Oats, and it became quickly apparent to me that we five existed somewhere in a world where we were definitely still seated "below the salt" at the business table. But it was a world in which we were also unwelcome at the secretarial tables in the corporate lunchroom. The men avoided sitting with us for fear of gossip, and the secretaries, who gossiped about us anyway, made it impossible for us to feel at ease in their presence. So some of us lunched together elsewhere in the building. Quaker Oats in those years occupied the second floor of the Merchandise Mart, and I often spent my lonely lunch hours roaming the upper floors of this megalith, looking in the windows of the furniture and fabric showrooms.

My fabulous life as a fledgling young executive took a nose dive at the end of the first year. Our small department was subsumed into the larger advertising division, whose newly appointed director, deciding to begin his regime with a tabula rasa, fired our entire department. Once the shock waves abated, I considered offers from several of the outside ad agencies whose client I had been. However, at that point, my father observed that as exciting as the advertising business had been, it was still only concerned with selling boxes off a shelf and not creating buildings. I am sure that, as a member of a profession that until only recently has scorned advertising as an undignified way of soliciting business, he was not pleased to see his eldest daughter about to delve more deeply into it. He suggested that I pack up my Vassar portfolio and visit Skidmore, Owings & Merrill. There I arrived as a prospective candidate for an entry-level position in the interiors department. Its head, Richard McKenna, had been sent to Chicago from the New York office. There he had worked under Davis Allen, the head of a group that designed the Chase Manhattan Bank interiors, among other notable commissions. Richard graciously accepted me as the newest team member and promptly assigned the task of designing a modern version of the recessed, spring-loaded coat hook that the more functionally inclined Adams West Lake Company of Chicago had produced for the Pullman Company's use in their railroad cars. I was allowed days to research and detail this singular object, symptomatic of Skidmore's concern for the design quality of the most minute element of its product portfolio.

I progressed to working under various established designers as I learned to use the Container Corporation of America's Color Harmony Manual, to recognize and specify suitable upholstery materials, to choose new colorways for them and design new weaves, to select elegant flitches for wood paneling, and to proportion and detail those panels appropriately, down to the smallest reveal between them. I was taught how to develop space plans based on program data I assembled and how to present those plans and materials to a client. Thus began my apprenticeship. I was fortunate, on the one hand, that the feminist revolution had begun and, on the other hand, that I had entered a profession considered natural for a woman. Nonetheless, in that most corporate of all architectural firms, I suffered the usual gender differential in wages and advancement. As with most women in the work force in those years, my stories of discrimination on and off the job are material for a novella. For instance, women on a construction site, as on a ship, were considered bad luck. There were always mutterings when I appeared and crossed fingers after I left, so that no accident would befall a worker until the memory of my visit had faded. This superstition did, however, give me great perverse power. No one in the field argued with me over construction details, lest I linger on the site longer than necessary.

It was a project in Nashville for the National Life and Accident Insurance Company that first brought me into contact with Davis Allen, the head of interiors in the New York office. Two years or so into my tenure at Skidmore, Owings & Merrill, Richard McKenna returned to the East Coast, leaving behind his protégé, an energetic and very ambitious designer named John Hornus, to whom I was assigned. The Nashville project was the most prestigious one in the office at the time because SOM's Chicago office was to design not only this corporate headquarters but also, under Davis Allen's direction, the furnishings for all thirty floors. By a series of events rife with office politics, John Hornus left the firm and I inherited the project.

Together Davis and I created the prototype for the full pedestal desk subsequently produced by the furniture manufacturers Steelcase and GF. A small book was published on Davis's work after he retired from the firm; the number of designers who learned from him and founded their own firms is legion. What influenced me most was his extraordinary flexibility as a designer. While staying within the modernist idiom of SOM, he was still able to introduce historicism. An eclectic who mixed new and old furnishings with ease, he captured the essential character of a client or place. In the case of National Life, the simple introduction of his elegantly designed English

oak louvers, inset in the high bronze-glass windows, brought a sense of the Southern to the travertine-clad high-rise. He found a weaver on Nantucket Island who wove rag fabrics from New York's Seventh Avenue into exquisitely unusual upholstery fabrics for the executive offices, and together we developed a

modern "Windsor" chair for them that became a substitute for the antiques they had originally requested. Years later Allen refined the chair further and named it the "Andover chair," after his prep school, selling it through the Stendig Furniture Company. It became the quintessential chair for designers working with transitional interiors because it personified traditional America recast into the twentieth century. It was his own fondness for American folk art that turned me into a collector, and his preference for the naive began to open my eyes to vernacular art and architecture worldwide.

Generally, on a headquarters building such as National Life, no expense was spared. The building module widened to six feet from the five-foot two-inch width used by Mies. This meant that all offices became larger, and bronze rather than stainless became the building's standard. Even the furniture had bronze legs or bronze trim, and veneers such as English brown oak were used for paneling as well as furnishings (the striking warm brown shade of the wood occurred because the tree was blighted). Even more rare than this straight-grained oak

were the burl and crotch-wood varieties. The straight grain was used for doors and panels, the burl for desks and cabinets. Offices were customized: for one executive, I designed a bronze case to house two porcelain Doughty birds from his collection. To hold the collection of medals won by another officer's

springer spaniel in field trials, we constructed a bronze display table that doubled as a coffee table.

For the general office art program, we introduced the idea of a collection of black-and-white photographs of

people and places taken by a professional photographer in all the states in which the insurance company had branch offices. Shel Hirshorn of Blackstar in New York was selected, and my assignment was to accompany him on his Tennessee leg. We set off from Memphis at dawn that first morning in August of 1969, intending to cross the state from west to east. But our first detour took us west across the Mississippi River into the peanut fields of Arkansas, where Shel attempted to photograph bandana-clad field workers who resisted being photographed. As we sat by the side of the river later that morning, eating a lunch of catfish and chips at a local fish house, Shel told me that he was also a known Civil Rights photographer and a marked man below the Mason-Dixon line. He warned me that we needed to be very careful to avoid any skirmishes with the law, such as falling into any of the speed traps that were often set up in small towns. "Once they learn my name, I'll be jailed without habeas corpus," he predicted. Thus began a week of adventure as we carefully crisscrossed the state. I had my camera with me and learned invaluable lessons from this pro as we rose at dawn every day and drove into the back country. He had a self-preservation instinct bar none and could sniff out the presence of a hidden still or a speed trap with equal ease. By the time we reached Knoxville to photograph the TVA dams along the Tennessee River, I had stored up unforgettable impressions of life in the South. After his assignment was completed that fall, it fell to me to become his editor and to make the final selections.

For all the travertine-clad building's fine finishes, it was built according to the famous SOM fast-track method, which meant that a construction management company was initially hired to budget the base building with allowances for the interior. Construction had begun with only shell and core drawings complete, and the entirety of the interior architectural package was designed and detailed while the building was under construction. This procedure saved time and of course money, shortening as it did the length of time required for the construction loan. What this method meant for me was that the interior design work ran concurrently with the architectural design, and so I was privy to all those processes. I traveled to Nashville with the architectural team and sat in on all the meetings during which the building was designed. All of the team members became my mentors. I

felt reasonably equal to my male counterparts until we traveled south together and stayed overnight. Checking into the hotel or motel was always an experience, since the desk clerk invariably assigned me to a room in as remote a spot as he could possibly find. Once I was even given the vacant room of a motel owner's daughter, a college student, because it was located behind the front desk, where he stood guard through the night. We all laughed at this absurd behavior, but it wasn't really very funny, indicative as it was of attitudes in the South toward women professionals. There were no female executives in the insurance company, either.

National Life was the last major office building that SOM designed that did not embrace the new "office landscape" theories that were drifting across the ocean from Europe, primarily Germany. As these theories slowly infiltrated SOM or were embraced by our clients, we became involved with office systems. The demise of the closed office and the rise of the open office system created opportunities to design work stations that operated like housing units for workers and were grouped into communities. To negotiate typical office floors of tall partitions laid out by facilities engineers was to enter a rabbit warren that reduced workers to the level of rodents. So I took on the cause of developing systems that freed workers from these cages. SOM, as often as it could, created its own designs. For Baxter Laboratories, I convinced client and architect that height differences between men and women were such that the ability to see over the top was the difference between psychological freedom and a sense of imprisonment. Our specially designed partitions were built under five feet in height. Years later, in my own practice, I designed many showrooms for two office-systems manufactur-

ers, Herman Miller and Haworth. For each I assembled "offices" configured to introduce a sense of whimsy into the work place, stretch the imaginations of the design community, and speak aesthetically to the issue of a humane working environment.

In general, at SOM I tended to be assigned to large-scale projects that lasted for several years. For nine of the eleven years that I worked there, these projects happened to bridge the several mini-recessions that occurred during that time, so I managed to escape the major layoffs that took place whenever work slowed. Unfortunately, as in Russian roulette, in the fall of 1975 the bullet filled the firing chamber. I had requested my first six-week leave of absence in late spring of that year (having accumulated an unheard-of number of vacation days) to take myself on an abbreviated grand tour. Upon my return in July, I received my next assignment, the interiors of the Holiday Inn Mart Plaza, located on the top floors of the SOM-designed Apparel Center, adjacent to the Merchandise Mart. The inn's budget was as small as their aspirations were large. The guest-room furnishings were to be selected with a shelf life of seven years—at which time they would be discarded. The bars, restaurants, and assembly rooms fared no better. This was obviously the antithesis of an SOM interior, but the country was in a recessionary period, and since the interiors department had already been downsized, the firm pursued the work. When it was awarded, my fate was sealed. Coincidentally, that August I was also put on a friend's list of potential dates for Stanley Tigerman, who had separated from his second wife that same spring.

It fell to me to invent ways of convincing the regional manager of the Holiday Inn that just because he had never seen anything like what we were proposing did not mean that our designs would be a failure. I also had to confront the inn's desire to provide suspended baskets in which bar patrons could sit and swing. This I did by my assertion that in this year of the miniskirt, women's stockings were particularly vulnerable to

wicker. I was able to substitute the idea of obtaining clothing labels from showrooms in the Apparel Center below, which would be placed under glass in this bar, entitled "Mad Anthony's." The name's association with apparel escaped all of us. Having stayed in many hotels of this type, with their flocked wallpaper and shag rugs, I took very seriously my charge to improve standards. For the rooms, I designed every item of furnishings from carpets to casements to cabinetry. They were restful places with quiet palettes. I even hired a photographer to take panoramic pictures of Illinois prairies and farms and of the Lake Michigan

sand dunes. These were printed by a billboard company in a ten-foot-by-eighteen-inch size and were framed to hang horizontally over the twin beds. In my crusade to make this the flagship for all Holiday Inns, I even designed the china and the service wardrobes. *Interiors* magazine put a picture of the lobby on the cover of their June issue in 1977 and published an eight-page article on the project. But by then the trigger had been pulled in this game of roulette, and my life at SOM was over, a victim of the continuing recession, the in-house criticism of the non-Miesian character of the hotel, and the depar-

ture from the firm of my principal mentor.

It never occurred to me to look for a similar position. To be a senior interior designer at SOM was the pinnacle of that particular, rather rarefied professional society. Instead I announced to what few friends

remained after these last purges that I was opening up my own practice. This I did on April Fool's Day of 1977, the same day I elected to leave SOM. I had been moonlighting the previous few years in an effort to augment my salary. Working nights and weekends on apartment interiors in the neighborhood, I had amassed a small clientele. With my architectural training, I was able to bridge the gap between the two professions and so became much in demand. I founded my own corporation—lodged in my efficiency apartment in one of Mies's Lake Shore Drive buildings—learned how to keep books, and hired interior design students from the University of Cincinnati's work/study program (which exchanged coop students every three months) on the chance that my fledgling enterprise wouldn't fly. But I had no official credentials, and so I set out to get some. I signed up for the exam required by the American Society of Interior Designers for professional membership. I failed the design portion of the NCIDQ the first time around because I failed to finish the assignment. I was too caught up in Skidmore-ish issues, worrying about minuscule proportional details, tracing reveals, and striving for a level of perfection unattainable within the time constraints. Six months later, when I sat for it again, I solved the problem in half the time allotted. The realities of a sole practitionership had taught me to assess a problem directly and to act upon it expeditiously.

With the initials ASID after my name, I then decided it was time to add AIA as well. Since eight of my years at SOM were enough to qualify me to take the architectural licensing exam under the now-defunct apprenticeship clause, my father had begun to strongly encourage me to take the exam. I contacted my former SOM mentors and they signed the requisite documents. I then signed up for the refresher course at the University of

Illinois in Chicago. After the first lecture on structures (vectors and their like), I was ready to throw in the towel. But it turned out that I had absorbed enough intuitive knowledge without recourse to mathematical formulas. I was able to pass that part of the exam, and the other sections fell into place quite naturally. After five days of tests, it was all over. The results came in the mail two months later. I was an architect, and Stanley and I celebrated by setting a wedding date.

In 1977, when I launched myself, I was adept at designing modern interiors. I had never been extremely comfortable copying the Miesian aesthetic and had become more confident in my own abilities. The direction in which I now went was decided by circumstances: the kinds of clients that chose to hire me, the places that I traveled to, the people that I met, and the architecture that I saw and studied. It was also decided by relationships. The central one is that with my husband Stanley Tigerman, who endlessly challenges me, as I do him, to become the best that I can be. Our creative natures are, of course, quite different, and when we design jointly—generally at the request of a client who knows us well—there are skirmishes, but the results are quite satisfying. In spite of Stanley's persuasive personality, I have forged and held fast to my own path, one influenced in part by the places I have been.

As a young designer at SOM, I had found myself returning most often on vacations to the East where I was educated, especially to New England, to the orderly towns along the Atlantic seaboard such as those in Maine, where the sea captain's white clapboard houses with their romantic widows' walks stand in stalwart symmetry, foursquare to the ocean winds and waves. I collected scrimshaw, the carved-ivory folk art of the sailors, and I sailed on schooners on Penob-

scott Bay. Colonial America's built response to adverse environments intrigued me. Whether many of the antecedents had a European affinity in their forms or not, it was the purposefulness of the architecture that had meaning for me. The inland farms of Vermont and New Hampshire, for example, are handsome complexes that aligned their front entrances along the post road and then stepped the attached outbuildings back from it. Although most of these farms, with their attached barns, had been adapted to become live-in antique shops, that did not alter their original purpose in providing a safe passage for the owner to care for stock in inclement climates. Much of the furnishing had that same purposeful character, especially the Shaker pieces, those elegant elemental objects that crossed the border into art.

Later, when my own practice allowed me more freedom to expand my study of American vernacular architecture, I also traveled farther south along the coast. In Charleston, I saw rows of houses that set their narrow facades toward the street and progressed backward in plan to take advantage of the prevailing breezes blowing off the harbor. The fact that the citizens were also taxed for the amount of property that abutted the street was another practical reason for their conformation. The covered porches and louvered colonnades that protected the interior from the western sun found parity in house forms farther inland. Houses of the rural South were constructed with paired living quarters bracketing a central covered breezeway used for assembly. These were nicknamed dog trots. This same environmental resolution—the Bernoulli principle of air movement, that is, the compressing of air to energize it and thereby increase its velocity—appeared in larger plantation homes, whose architects designed wide interior hallways that were open at each end; these hall-

ways drew the air from flanking rooms, cooling them. Another adaptation of this principle was the construction of a central stair tower that culminated in an open cupola, causing the warm air to rise up and out (the so-called stack effect). Modern mechanical systems have caused the demise of many of America's most interesting vernacular buildings. Those that are still copied are produced as shells, their inner workings altered to reflect concerns of the moment rather than climatic ones. I was determined whenever possible to convince my clients to adopt principles of passive environmental control and to allow these ideas to inform the character of the work.

European architectural study began with my solo grand tour the spring of 1975 when I took my six-week sabbatical from SOM. I concentrated on the British Isles. In London, I found in the rooms of Sir John Soane's eigh-

teenth-century museum in Lincoln's Inn Fields a richness of spatial layers within minimal dimensions. I marveled at his taut surfaces and pure geometries, and the economy of means used to achieve them. The minimalism that appears as the precursor of modernism, and a sense of his underlying primitivism, struck a chord that vibrated in me. In the countryside I found more affinity with the Cotswold-stone classical buildings that formed the crescent in Bath than I did with the half-timbered Gothic ones that ambled about Stratford-upon-Avon. I felt closer to those country estates that stood apart in nature, ordered and serene, than to those that joined the natural randomness, and yet I loved to stumble upon the ad hoc industrial structures of the Cornish tin mines that reared their heads above the high hedgerows bordering all the roads in Cornwall. On the Wilshire chalk plain the massive stones in the Druid Circle of Stonehenge plucked some

Gaelic string wired deep within me as I watched the sun rise over the keystone on the summer solstice. I longed to express in my own work the same elemental power of that primitive geometrical clock.

After roaming through the endless rooms of enormous estates in England, I related to the more diminutive scale of those in Scotland. Their modest size seemed most like their American suburban counterparts. I was amazed by the elegant interiors of Charles Rennie Mackintosh, who exerted artistic control over every aspect of the interior. Never has

white enameled furniture attained such stature. In Ireland, I mourned the loss of the whitewashed stone cottages I had expected to see and wondered why the bright pastels that they had been painted looked so natural in southern climes yet so unnat-

ural on a gray Irish day. But the strong deep colors of the town house doors in the squares of Dublin seemed appropriate, set as they were in gray stone facades; the ordered classical facade of Castletown, on the outskirts of the city, presided in isolated splendor over pastoral gardens.

I had landed in England at the start of a hot, dry spring, and by the time I reached Ireland there was a serious drought. The Emerald Isle had turned brown. The roads were dusty, and signs in hotels requesting tourists not to bathe began to appear. Flies were everywhere, and I was reminded of the potato crop failure that had sent my great-great-grandfather McCurry and his brothers fleeing to America in the 1860s. I looked for the three brothers in the parish record books in Killarney, in County Kerry, and in the countryside around MacGillycuddy's Reeks (our pre–Ellis Island name), but none were to be found. Apparently my dad

had not remembered the correct county; it was Cork, I discovered later. (I had forgone the search for my mother's Scotch-Irish ancestors, the Bells, because of the troubles in Northern Ireland.) Suddenly, I felt very alone and foreign. Maybe it was just that this search for my roots was the culmination of six weeks of wandering with only my single-lens-reflex camera for company, but I was not unhappy to feel the tug of America and to return home in time for the bicentennial celebration on July 4. A month later I reconnected with Stanley Tigerman and our courtship began.

Four years later, in March of 1979, I was back in Europe, this time on a honeymoon doubling as a lecture tour. The architectural influences and examples that I had experienced on my earlier trip were now augmented by visits with architects themselves, as friends in every country showed us their work and passed us on to new friends. To avoid disputes brought on by the differential between the time it took for me to take a photograph versus the time it took for Stanley to make a drawing, I learned to lead him to the center of a town square and to leave him there with his sketchbook while I wandered around the town, soaking up all it had to offer. Stanley never seemed to mind that he usually only saw part of every city or town, as long as he filled his notebooks with sketches that he would complete on trains or planes or over drinks in outdoor cafés and then give away to friends or clients or trade to other architects.

Throughout the next ten years, we traveled extensively. We spent the spring of 1980 living in Rome, where Stanley was the architect in residence at the American Academy. The neoclassical McKim, Mead and White palazzo on the Via Angelo Masina sat on top of the Janiculum, one of the seven hills of Rome. The Academy was bounded on one side by a brick wall of the ancient city, which now enclosed formal gardens and a clay tennis court. Our apartment had been McKim's own and looked out over these same gardens. With Rome spread out below us, we indulged in a movable feast. Mornings were spent in the Academy library, but we ventured out every afternoon, descending to the city below and passing on the way Bramante's *tempietto* in the courtyard of San Pietro in Montorio, adjacent to the Spanish Academy. Sated at the end of the day, we caught the bus at the Largo Argentina and were carried back up the hill to dinner in the jasmine-scented courtyard, followed by a concert, a reading, or a game of cowboy billiards. Near the end of our stay

we traveled to the Veneto with James Ackerman, the Palladian scholar from Harvard who was also in residence and had just finished a book on the *palazzi* of the Veneto. We toured, sketched, and photographed all the work of Palladio and his contemporaries and had dinner on the lawn of Malcontenta with the Foscaris, two married architects teaching history at the University of Venice, whose family had commissioned the villa in the sixteenth century.

We each sketched or photographed buildings we wished to remember. My collection included the Roman

Forum, for its obvious significance as the center of Greco-Roman civilization; Hadrian's Pantheon, ca. 130 CE, for its mathematical mysteries and monumentality; Cerveteri, the seventh-century BCE Etruscan necropolis outside Rome, with its family burial

chambers sculpted from soft rock, miniature residences with small stone seats carved out for familial visitations; the small medieval church at Spoleto near the Duomo, for its powerfully elemental Romanesque interior; Poiana, a smaller Palladian villa; and Palladio's La Rotonda, for the strength of its symmetrical plan and

dominance of its site, its windows presenting controlled vistas of the surrounding hills.

After the glories of Rome had faded somewhat, I settled back to work in my small office in the efficiency apartment that had been my home before we married. Coincidentally, both Mies buildings were condominiumized shortly before our marriage; I bought my apartment for my office and moved to the building next door to share Stanley's one-bedroom, which has since grown through two annexations to occupy one sunny end of the top floor looking east over the lake and south and west across the city.

Rome seemed to mark a turning point in the affairs of Margaret I. McCurry, Ltd. I had spent the previous three years building an interior architecture practice that included the requisite number of residential remodelings, furnishings, and condominium lobbies designed for clients recommended to me by my original moonlighting group when I was still at SOM. I had also developed several institutional clients during that time. Several executive women at the South Shore Bank hired me to remodel the cafeteria after I had worked on an apartment interior for one of them. Eight years later, in 1988, when I was invited to join the Chicago Network, part of the International Women's Forum, I renewed my acquaintance with them.

My small practice also got a boost from associating with other architects. Stanley, of course, very interested in my survival, supported me with several interior-design commissions. I refurnished the lobby of his Miesian-inspired Boardwalk Apartment building and worked with him on a couple of residences, including one in the John Hancock Building. Through him I also came to know and work with many members of the Chicago Seven. This group of architects took their name from the original Chicago Seven, a group of Vietnam War dissidents. A publication entitled *100 Years of Chicago Architecture* had connected the original Chicago school with Mies, leaving out a number of significant early Chicago architects in the process, including Andrew Rebori, my father's early employer in the 1930s, and George Fred Keck, Stanley's first employer in the 1950s. Stanley assembled several associates—Larry Booth, Stuart Cohn, and Ben Weese—and together they created a revisionist exhibition (which opened at the Cooper Union in New York) and book entitled *Chicago Architects*. The outgrowth of that assemblage, adding to its ranks Tom Beeby, James Ingo Freed (then dean at the Illinois Institute of Technology), and James Nagle, became the Chicago Seven. The seven then expanded to eleven with the inclusion of Helmut Jahn, Ken Schroeder, Cynthia Weese, and Gerald Horn. This group later revived

the Chicago Architectural Sketch Club, first formed at the turn of the century, which I was invited to join in 1982.

In 1980, Jim Nagle hired me to do the interiors of a promotional house he had designed for U.S. Gypsum, and five years later we associated again on the remodeling of the Park Ridge Country Club in the suburbs, whose clubhouse had been designed by Hugh Garden of my father's firm, Schmidt, Garden & Erickson, after the original wooden one by Frank Lloyd Wright burned to the ground. Before I left for Rome Cynthia Weese had brought me in to help her with the interiors of a residence she had designed in the western suburbs and, as our friendship grew, invited me to join the awards committee of the Chicago chapter of the AIA in 1982. Over the course of the next seven years we became board members; she rose to the presidency, and I followed as vice president. Weese eventually moved on to the national board, while I chose to devote more energies to the national AIA Committee on Design (COD), for which we had both been recruited in 1984. This group within the ranks of the AIA was founded by Jean Paul Carlhian of Shepley Bulfinch in 1968 to ensure that aesthetics remained in the forefront of the AIA's policies. Stanley spent a number of years on the committee, chairing it in 1976, and I became its twenty-fifth chair in 1993, the first woman to hold that position.

In the years following our return from Rome, my commissions increased, as did my professional commitments. I had progressed to permanent employees, but still kept my own corporate books. One evening after dinner Stanley's son, Judson, who was living with us while he searched for his first job, watched me pore over the ledgers and suggested that his father put me out of my bookkeeping miseries by offering me a partnership in his firm. We debated this novel notion and agreed to merge our two separate firms into one. So on a subzero day in

January 1982, I relocated down the street to Stanley's firm, housed in an old seven-story former apartment building at 920 North Michigan Avenue. The un-air-conditioned top floor, once a ballroom, was painted yellow and sported french doors that opened onto the avenue; the domed ceiling was inscribed with a five-foot-long Mongol HB pencil. Magritte-like clouds were painted on the dome, and slow-moving ceiling fans revolved continuously. On hot summer days, when, for survival, we cranked up their speed, the vortex caused the drawings to levitate. Stanley had also simultaneously offered partnership to his associate Robert Fugman. For five years the firm was a triumvirate until, after several successful Hard Rock Cafés were produced by Bob as the managing partner, he departed with that client in tow to set up his own practice. After that, it was just the two of us.

I began a ten-year remodeling relationship with the Saddle & Cycle Club, an organization that incorporated at the turn of the century as a riding, cycling, and swimming club located on the lakefront at the northern edge of the city. The fill for Lake Shore Drive eventually landlocked the club, but it continued on, trading the beach and stables of yesteryear for a nine-hole golf course and a slew of tennis courts. There was always an ever-changing building or decorating committee to work with, and out of those complex interrelationships grew further commissions. At the end of the first years of association, I was approached by one member of the club's building committee, a real-estate broker. He was also a board member of the Juvenile Protective Association (JPA). After procuring a building site for the JPA, he persuaded the board to hire me to design their headquarters by convincing them that anyone who could handle the diverse personalities represented by the Saddle & Cycle Club's committees could deal with them as well. This was the first project I brought into the firm as Stanley's partner. For the next fifteen years, without ever a thought for specialization, I continuously worked with one town or country club or another. They have all had original buildings designed by some of the best architectural firms in the city, from D. H. Burnham to Holabird & Root, which I restored, remodeled, or added to.

The first year of our partnership, Stanley and I collaborated on the design of a tea service for Alessi, the Italian manufacturer of tableware,

whose factory is located in Crusinello, near Milan. We had visited Alberto Alessi's estate on Lago Dorta two years before when we were in Italy for the Venice Biennale and had discussed his plans to have a number of international architects design these sets. They were to be produced first in sterling silver for exhibition and then in stainless steel for mass consumption. Michael Graves was already working on his famous whistling tea kettle. One weekend in the summer of 1981 when we were driving to Elkhart Lake, Wisconsin, in my old Fiat Spyder to visit Stanley's daughter, Tracy, at camp, we started to discuss what

form these objects should take. As I recall, Stanley was interested in anthropomorphic forms and I was arguing for Euclidean geometries. We compromised and combined the two ideas into some shapes that were spheres and cylinders, but that had body parts for handles or other supports. The silver exhibition collection was displayed around the country and at the Museum of Contemporary Art in Chicago, where Joan and Irving Harris, our friends and clients, purchased all twelve architects' designs. We tried to convince the Italians that our service was a collaboration and should be credited as such, but they continually left off the McCurry part in the exhibition and in subsequent publications, and the set has for many years been attributed solely to Stanley. This incident confirmed my sense that my credibility and identity as an independent architect needed to be further established and strengthened. I began to focus more exclusively on my own projects. This strategy prevailed with just one exception—our own weekend cottage—for the first five years of our partnership.

These past fifteen or so years have produced some memorable designs. I have reconstructed twenty-five of them as "short stories" for this book, because an architect's story is essentially incomplete without an alter ego. Architects are not conventional artists alone with figurative canvases. Our art requires a client as a component in the act of creation. These stories start with my first architectural collaboration with Stanley, our cottage, and end with a solo commission completed as the century draws to a close. These texts are not distillations of the design idea; they chronicle the evolution of the design process, delineating the relationships that have formed as circles of friendship and referrals spread out over the years. That has been the traditional way of practicing, fitting perhaps for a traditional architect.

Sometimes in retrospect, as I contemplate the place I have in the architectural scheme of things, I think of Robert Frost and his poem "The Road Not Taken." I think of the more heavily traveled road and how I took the "road less traveled by." I have had a good view of the former road; I have seen theoretical movements begin with great power and authority and then, as they are codified, lapse into styles. I have watched careers skyrocket, only to note that their upward trajectory is in direct symmetry with their downward spiral. The projects included here testify to my belief that taking one's own road, rather than racing around another's, is in the end the most satisfying and steady course.

BOARDWALK

*Lakeside, Michigan
1982–83*

I began to have visions of a country place during the eleven years I lived in my 450-square-foot efficiency apartment at 900 North Lake Shore Drive. Since it was one of a pair of Mies van der Rohe's glass towers, the size was mitigated somewhat by its twenty-by-eight-foot glass curtain wall. When Stanley Tigerman and I married, we lived in his top-floor one-bedroom apartment in the adjacent building. The square footage was slightly better, but still the land beckoned. A house in the suburbs was never an option. We were both happy to live two blocks away from our office.

For the first three summers of our marriage we were invited to stay in the "House That Bob (Stern) Built" in East Hampton. Stanley's excuse for not building had been his conviction that good architects couldn't stray far from their offices. He relented at the end of the third summer. And so the search for a place began. I drew a circle approximately one and a half hours of driving time out from around the city center, and we circumnavigated its circumference on a number of weekends, one fall finally settling on the dune lands of Lake Michigan's southeastern shore, just north of the Indiana border—a backwater place of somewhat shabby towns and small resorts that were populated by Chicagoans in the first half of the century but neglected after World War II, when gas prices became reasonable once again and the automobile took the summer people farther north in search of cooler nights. Aware of the dangers of two architects married to each other attempting to design their own home, let alone on a shoestring budget, we decided to search instead for the quintessential Michigan cottage.

This area, now nicknamed Harbor Country by the joint Chambers of Commerce of the six or so communities that comprise it, has since been rediscovered. But early in 1982, the price of real estate reflected its decline and we were shown a number of properties with varying degrees of

potential. Union Pier had a large stock of shabby bungalows, the frame versions of brick counterparts found in older Chicago neighborhoods. We even found one faded complex, the Rainbow Cove Resort, up for sale. Its seven cabins with gabled front porches were clustered in a semicircle around a cracked concrete patio with a flagpole stuck in its center. As I inspected each unit, not so secretly coveting the old white wicker furniture set out on each porch, Stanley fantasized about buying the resort, keeping the center cabin, and selling off the remaining six to the other members of the Chicago Seven. It was a shortlived vision.

We saw several other such neglected properties that fit into our small budget that fall, and with each Stanley would enthusiastically explore their potential for transformation. The most farfetched prospect to come under his scrutiny was a two-story concrete-block garage sitting beside a dirt road in Union Pier. It was painted a dull rose but had rather well-pro-

portioned doors. Stanley insisted that this relic could easily be transformed into its European counterpart—the stuccoed gatehouse standing alongside the high street at the village entrance. Fortunately, before the snow fell, but not before the football season ended, we abandoned the Sunday afternoon cottage search since none had survived extant and settled for an empty acre a block from the beach in Lakeside, the adjoining small town to the north.

In my mind I had always pictured my brother-in-law's family cottage in Pentwater, Michigan, when I conjured up images of a summer place—a white clapboard box perched on a high dune overlooking the lake. It had no significant architectural features except for a straightforward plan. At either end of the central living/dining room, were pairs of bedrooms. Their doorways opened onto this main room, where everyone settled around the wood-burning stove on cold summer evenings. At night, curled up under camp blankets, one listened to

the quiet of nature and the sounds of family, the squeaking of springs on the old iron bedsteads, the rustling of book pages of the late-night readers, the coals hissing in the grate.

And so this became the Lakeside plan—albeit imbued with the idea of an outdoor piazza as the central gathering space, abutted by pairs of interior rooms at either end and overlooked by balconied sleeping lofts. All this was to fit within a footprint of eight hundred square feet—an economical twenty-by-forty-foot box. It would need to accommodate visiting friends as well as Stanley's children and their extended family.

Interested always in an architecture subject to multiple interpretations, and in this case one that evoked associations with archetypal rural forms as well as historical references, we designed the house as a barn with monitors or a basilica with clerestories. The granary porch became a baptistry with a stock silo roof. At the same time, industrial galvanized metal brought forth memories of the Indiana steel works that line the bottom of the lakeshore, bisected by the Chicago Skyway—the direct motor route for Chicagoans through Indiana to the Michigan shore.

The house was built primarily by one cabinetmaker, the husband of the agent who found the property for us. Rich Brychta was a quiet soul who must have come to dread Monday mornings when we would get up at dawn to drive around the lake for the weekly inspection. Since the so-called working drawings were nothing more than a basic design set for the simple permit required by the township, the actual construction decisions were made collaboratively at these Monday sessions.

In our lectures, we present the house somewhat differently. Stanley prefers to refer to it as an industrial extrusion arbitrarily chopped off at the ends and gridded. I liken the shift to lattice grid from corrugated steel to Eastern antecedents that expressed either their

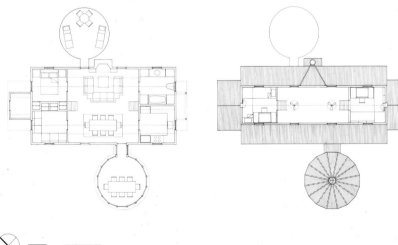

0   5   10   20 ft

individuality or their parsimony by shifting from shingled front and rear elevations that matched their shake roof to clapboard or stone ends.

When it won an AIA Honor Award its first year, we amused the audience of architects at the convention by structuring the acceptances so that I accepted for the architect and Stanley for the client. Vincent Scully wrote an article on it for *Architectural Digest*, and Susan Doubilet, a staff writer from *Progressive Architecture*, also did an article on the house. Since the latter piece tipped our carefully balanced scales toward Stanley, I was disappointed by her lack of objectivity.

We named the house "Boardwalk" partially because of its elevated walkway but also as a reference to Monopoly's highest rental—a name that Stanley had also given to his first high-rise apartment building. Today, Stanley is still to be found inside, away from nature in the screened silo, while I garden until all hours even in the dead of winter. Stanley will, on occasion, venture tentatively out to the folly by the fishing pond that terminates the boardwalk. Every year or so the urge to build something on our acre overcomes him. I add flower beds and he plans constructions. The latest is a Schinkelesque arbor—a rebar grid that arcs over the lower arm of the pond over which I am training rambling roses. The arbor was built in memory of one that Karl Friedrich Schinkel designed for the royal palace Sanssouci in Potsdam, which Stanley saw during a trip to Germany. For each of us this house is an important expression of the individual search for our distinct voices. Its form is one that reappears again and again in both of our bodies of work. Its plan has become a paradigm for me: the axis and cross axis that are established through doorways and windows extend one's perception into the natural world and relate inside to out.

SUHU GALLERY

Chicago, Illinois
1982–83

Coincidentally, two clients with whom I worked continuously during my tenure as a sole proprietor were related. One brother, the younger, owned a print gallery. We had become acquainted over the years that I assembled corporate art collections at SOM. The older brother controlled the family business, a chemical company located on the near west side of the city. For five years I alternated between furnishing the younger's residence and remodeling the elder's business. And then in the early 1980s, when all the art galleries began a mass exodus from the high-rent district that

North Michigan Avenue had become, I was commissioned by my dealer client to convert eight thousand square feet of commercial loft space into a gallery. Most of the galleries had opted to move west eight blocks to an area filled with brick factory buildings between Superior and Huron Streets, subsequently dubbed Suhu in a less than subtle reference to New York's Soho district.

My client, who aspired to expand his business from works on paper to the whole gamut of artistic expression, selected the largest building in the complex, which was also the westernmost, to maximize

his dollar-per-square-foot spatial opportunities. This Chicago warehouse block built in the 1880s was reputed to have been designed by Louis Sullivan. For us its strongest feature was its requisite twelve-foot ceilings and repetitive modules. The heavy-timber structural system expressed itself in a nineteen-by-thirteen-foot bay that was defined by square knee-braced posts that supported wooden beams, which in turn tied back into the exterior masonry bearing wall. The commercial loft building may have served its light industrial clients well for over seventy-five years but in the process it had taken considerable abuse.

As I set pencil to paper I was aware of my challenge: to make art while making a suitable place for art. What I determined to do was to convince the art dealer to accept the parameters of the column spacing, which when enclosed dictated eighteen-foot-wide galleries, rather than to insist on wider galleries that would contain exposed columns. I envisioned encasing in planes of drywall those closely spaced posts whose knee braces flared out at the awkward height of eight feet. I intended to create connecting rooms in order to intentionally reference the sequential planning of traditional museum spaces. This was not the type of space that lent itself to slipped and floating wall planes artfully disposed in space, like other galleries in neighboring buildings that had larger bays and taller columns. To prepare my case I made a careful analysis of the maximum widths of competitors' display spaces. I needed first to assure my client that eighteen feet, the maximum width of an enclosed column bay, was wide enough to adequately display larger works of art. The competitors' averaged twenty feet. I built a foam-core

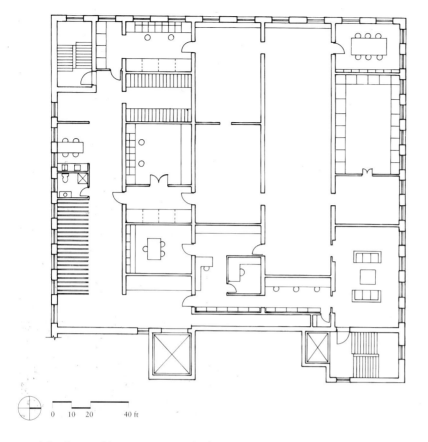

0 10 20   40 ft

model of movable partitions, which we moved backward and forward for many days. It took considerable discussion for us to agree on the design scheme, which followed the structural system by sheathing the posts in linear stretches of drywall, thus dividing the floor along the post lines into five long eighteen-foot-wide bays that were then transversely and intermittently spanned by other walls. The plan basically and with very simple economies organized the rooms into a classical processional system of suites, whereby clientele circulated from room to room through deep connecting doorways aligned with each other, so that vistas existed through the entire suite. This plan, while influenced by my Roman sabbatical, was primarily the result of my studies as an art-history major of which settings most promoted the comfortable contemplation of art. What I concluded was that there existed a proportional relationship between the size of the room and the

size and location of the entry into or exit from it. In other words, to focus foremost on experiencing the work of art, viewers needed to feel that, on the one hand, there was a comprehensible processional system through which they could move, but, on the other hand, they also needed to feel that enough enclosure existed around them to ensure a sense of security and relative solitude for a one-on-one confrontation with the art. What I conceived of was the creation of a miniature museum. Traditional spaces would be proportionally reduced in size to signify the scale of a gallery, but the plan would have a logic and clarity similar to that of a museum. Thus the rooms were of different lengths but were always eighteen feet wide. When spaces required privacy, french doors with adjustable venetian blinds were installed, so that one always sensed space or light on the other side. The sales rooms were organized so that clients entered directly from the gal-

leries into quiet, air-conditioned spaces with soft seating and soft lights that also had direct access to the storage areas in the rear for a constant flow of readily available purchasable art.

The gallery also generated revenue by becoming a popular rental venue for parties. The Chicago Architectural Club held its annual party in the gallery in 1986, and a wedding was logged in the visitors' register. Most of these events occurred in the fall, since the slow-moving ceiling fans that cooled the gallery spaces could not cope with summer crowds. With my client acting as general contractor, the project was constructed and furnished for twelve dollars per square foot. It was cited by the Chicago chapter of the AIA in their 1983 awards program and won the "Big I" award from *Interiors* magazine the same year for best in low-budget design.

But times change, and eventually the rents in Suhu began to rise. In the spring of 1989 the recession had moved westward from the East Coast, the bottom was dropping out of the art market, and many galleries were contemplating moving again, this time farther west across the Chicago River. This was a far riskier move, because it was no longer in walking distance of North Michigan Avenue and thus meant an end to much of the walk-in tourist trade. My client was reluctant to join the avant-garde group that relocated, partly because his business had remained with a more corporate clientele with offices in the Loop. Even as the notices were sent to those galleries that remained in the building that the structure had been sold and was to be converted into condominiums, my client stayed, protesting the cancellation of his lease while searching in vain for a comparable but smaller space that he could purchase in the same vicinity. By April, after the other galleries had moved out, he was alone in the

building, surrounded by workmen beginning the conversion process; then, early one morning, a suspicious fire broke out, completely destroying the structure. As I arrived at the office that same morning, I heard the continuous scream of sirens sounding to the north and west of our own loft building, located in the River North district some eight blocks southeast of Suhu. I sensed that it was the Sullivan building. I loaded my camera, slowly walked over to the conflagration, and took two pictures of the burning building. My client was standing on the pavement across the street, just apart from the crowds, watching streams of water from the firemen's hoses arcing hopelessly into the flames. We spoke briefly (I was building a house for him near Steamboat Springs, Colorado), but there was little we could say. He had stored many of his personal possessions in the space.

What now remains of my first

award-winning interior are two orthometric drawings and a rendered plan. The department of architecture at the Art Institute of Chicago asked me to donate those drawings to their permanent collection after the historian Bob Bruegmann wrote about them in *Inland Architect*:

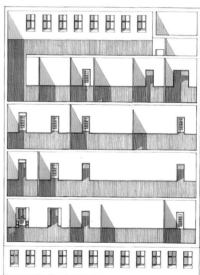

Once seen, the little drawing of the space seems almost inevitable. How could any other drawing record so perfectly the syncopated series of spaces? The simplicity of the drawings, the minimal means— black ink and Zipatone—make this sheet so clear and precise it seems almost surreal, a quality greatly enhanced by the seemingly diminutive scale and random placement of openings. How mysterious a world is created with such economy. This is the kind of drawing that transcends its function of describing a space and justifies the exhibition of architectural drawings in a museum of fine arts.

JUVENILE PROTECTIVE ASSOCIATION

*Chicago, Illinois
1983–84*

Following closely on my spatial studies of room proportions for the contemplation of art, I was presented with the challenge of designing a building to house the headquarters of a not-for-profit, privately funded agency, the Juvenile Protective Association (JPA). Rooms in this complex would be used not only for counseling but for reflecting on the results of counseling. They would belong to professionals who worked primarily in the field with dysfunctional families under difficult circumstances and then returned back to the office to what they hoped would be a quiet retreat between assignments.

The city lot that had been found for JPA was the result of a careful search for a neighborhood into which the agency would fit comfortably. It was close enough to many of its constituents and it was accessible to transportation. Best of all, it was located on Halsted, a street of mixed zoning that was also one of

the famous thoroughfares of Chicago, stretching from the northern to southern boundaries of the city and containing along its length almost every ethnic community in the city.

The 50-by-140-foot-deep commercial site meant that the building could be built out to the edge of the lot lines to maximize the amount of square footage in the footprint. What that also meant was that there would be no windows on the two demising walls of the structure. The lot was covered with a rubble fill from a razed building and dropped several feet below the raised street level. This condition indicated that the original buildings on the site had escaped the Great Chicago Fire of 1871 that swept northeastward through the city from the near southwest side, destroying most of the downtown and reaching farther north than this community but also farther east.

Before I began the conceptual drawings I discussed the parameters and the programming of the building with the board and the director, because it was self-evident in the association's not-for-profit status that the exigencies of the budget would be a significant factor in the design. We knew that the footprint was of a sufficient size to produce a single-story building that would include all the necessary personnel and support facilities planned, but with no room to spare. We then determined the priorities. It would be a clear-span building—the extra cost for this structural system was outweighed by the desire for a column-free space that would enhance the resale potential for the building should such a need arise. The bearing walls would be painted concrete block—the most economical material. The office walls would be extended up to the underside of the deck to minimize sound transmission and ensure privacy. For storage, it would have as much of a full basement as the budget would allow, but a large community assembly room would not be possible below because of the cost in square footage and dollars of providing required entrance and egress. Finally, we agreed that a portion of the rear of the lot would be dedicated to parking to satisfy codes as well as personnel. At the end of the discussion all the board members knew that the building would be a simple rectangular box. It would be up to me to design a facade that downplayed its institutionality to the neighborhood while simultaneously imparting a sense of the seriousness of its purpose to those clients who were counseled in the building.

But it was also up to me to create an interior environment that was conducive to counseling. It seemed appropriate to organize those areas requiring the most attendees at the front and to greet all guests from a

central location at a reception desk. An adjacent gazebo also served as a skylit children's playroom since the receptionist monitored that activity when parents were in counseling. At the rear, all the offices were delineated like small houses and grouped together like a village surrounding a skylit "courtyard"—the clerical enclosure. Those offices without actual outside windows shared this skylit enclave by means of their french doors or muntinized windows. To further downplay institutionality, the corridor ceilings were drywalled and the corridors were lit by sconces that bracketed doors or windows. Only in the offices was there an acoustical-tile ceiling and fluorescent lighting to produce the most practical and economical working environment. To explain our designs to the board we made a colored cardboard model and watercolor drawings of the plans and elevations, which were later requested for the archives of the department of architecture at the Art Institute.

Ground was broken in the fall of 1983. Nine months later, as the building neared completion, I learned that a donation of interior design services was needed. This was my first commercial building and I wanted to be involved in it in its entirety, so I discussed with Stanley committing our firm to this donation of services. He agreed, and I proceeded to contact furniture suppliers to either donate or discount their products. Knoll was one of the first to offer desk chairs at a reduced price, and since most of the desks were designed as built-ins and the millwork was also discounted we were able to stay within the modest budget. A board member donated the window coverings and we purchased posters for the art program from my Suhu Gallery.

The facade design was based on the eight-inch-square-scored con-

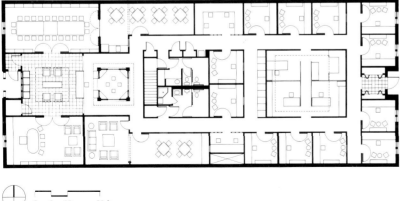

0   5   10   20 ft

crete-block wall of the building. Painted "pilasters" subdivided the gridded wall into three sections, which echoed the front room divisions in plan and the office/houses in elevation. An eight-by-eight-inch washable ceramic-tile field was made to adhere to the lower portion of the painted block, in order to protect it from the ravages of the ubiquitous spray-paint cans that cover many inner-city neighborhoods with graffiti. The same tile also repeated itself in a pattern on the floor in the lobby. Gridded windows, symmetrically disposed about the gridded doorway, reinforce the block pattern that begins with the geometry of the three squares. Only the semicircle of the graphics above the doorway introduces another geometrical shape and establishes an entrance hierarchy. The graphics were designed by Michael Glass as a conscious counterpoint. Four years after the JPA was completed, it won a Chicago chapter AIA award with Mack Scogin and Charles Moore on the jury.

Some eight years after the original JPA was commissioned, the director called to ask me to remodel a 1950s former light-industrial building into an adjunct facility that would concentrate its efforts on parent-infant research and development. This required observation and assembly rooms for family groups and more interactive work stations for staff. As in the original headquarters building, a sense of order and tranquillity prevails, with playful overtones. Front and back corridors are again organized like streets that pass by "houses" on their way to the playground at the end of the block. Not long after it opened, the recession deepened in Chicago and contributions to JPA followed the same downward spiral as the economy, until the institution was forced to retrench and close the doors on the new facility.

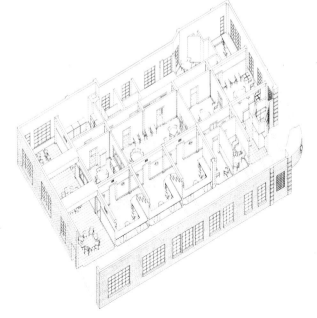

HERMAN MILLER

Chicago, Illinois
1984–86

Every June in Chicago, the con-tract-furniture industry introduces new products to the design and facilities professions at a national exposition with the acronym Neo-con. Held in the Merchandise Mart, a megalith of a building a city block square situated on the north bank of the east branch of the Chicago River, this event draws attendees from around the country who come to Chicago to tour the furniture showrooms and to listen to talks on subjects ranging from the state of the art of office systems to telecom-munications in the twenty-first cen-tury. During the economic boom of the 1980s, when owners and designers alike were riding on an optimistic bandwagon, furniture manufacturers either redesigned or, at the very least, refurnished their showrooms on a yearly basis. The design of these showrooms became a prized commission because, like the song, anything goes. So any-thing went, especially anything that

would signal a manufacturer's com-mitment to the expanding office-furniture market: as fast as archi-tects could design them and developers build them, high-rise office towers rose on city skylines. During that decade, internationally renowned architects from Michael Graves to Arata Isozaki had their moments in the showroom sun.

My own sunny moments began in 1984 and ended with the decade. I first dipped my fingers into the Neo-con pool when graphic designer Carol Naughton asked me to assist her with an assignment she had been given from Herman Miller to con-ceptualize and then accessorize their showroom for Neocon '84. This office-furniture manufacturer, which fabricated lines designed by the famous architects and industrial designers of the mid-twentieth cen-tury (Eero Saarinen and Charles Eames among them), decided to emphasize the civility of their com-pany by creating a user-friendly

showroom that would attract the weary consumers who had worn themselves out circumnavigating floors that in square footage equaled the size of the Pentagon. The idea was that the smell of fresh-roasting espresso would waft through the corridor, enticing those weary travelers into the showroom. Once there, they would sit at a coffee bar constructed of systems furniture and relax into the depths of an ergonomically correct executive office chair. Upended canvas umbrellas lighted from above cast an intimate glow over the libations.

Carol and I then conceived of other venues to hold the interest of our captured consumers. Working with Herman Miller's Facilities Design Group, we built a bookstore out of Action Office, the workhorse of the office-partition system, which had first been introduced while I was still at SOM. A striped awning in front announced that the Prairie Avenue Bookshop was selling vol-

umes on architecture and design. We resurrected Herman Miller's classic furniture pieces from their archives and upholstered them in fabrics designed by Alexander Girard to remind other designers of Herman Miller's history of support for the great designers of the past. This part was especially fun for me because in 1955 my father had furnished our Lake Forest house with many of these same classics, including Brazilian rosewood cabinetry and bedroom sets by Georg Nelson, drapery fabric by Alexander Girard, and of course the ubiquitous Saarinen lounge chair and ottoman. Carol and I also created vignettes in other work-station configurations to indicate what type of hip corporate executive might inhabit these offices. We succeeded so well in establishing a unique presence for the showroom that not only was Carol asked to do a repeat performance the following year but I was asked to design a setting in the rear

of the showroom for the introduction of Ethospace, a new office-systems product that would bow not at Neocon but in a special preview in the fall of 1984 that promised high visibility within the facilities world.

Based on the Greek word *ethos,* translating as the essential characteristics of a community or genus of a system, this product was the first partition system I had seen that had substantiality. The partitions were 3½ inches thick, thus having the dimensionality of walls. It eliminated that sense of insecurity and temporality often associated with the whole idea of working not in a constructed office but in a temporary office carrel. Ethospace was designed as a gridded steel framework of varying heights that not only supported files and work tops but was organized so that panels called tiles were attached to the frame in modulated increments. These tiles could be covered in acoustic fabric or glazed to act as windows, and they were interchangeable in the field, so that work stations could be customized for differing individuals with differing tasks. It created a sense of place, a home for workers in open offices. As I contemplated how to design an architectural setting that would convey this image, I thought of Joseph Rykwert's book *Adam's House in Paradise,* which discussed humankind's primeval home, and I decided to re-create that idea of originality to show that Ethospace was part of a timeless continuum of place-making. Using the twenty-by-twenty-foot concrete bay of the Merchandise Mart as the basis for a Cartesian grid, I wrapped the columns in ordinary concrete block, using split-face block at the base to signify rustication. I inset gravel-colored carpets into a "stone" floor grid that shadowed the overhead beams, which were supported on the columns. The hollow beams held an uplighting cove, negating the need for fluorescent lights in the nine-foot-high acoustical-tile ceiling of the existing showroom. The cove also created an illusion of infinite space above the ceiling grid. I then used a single wythe of block to subdivide the perimeter of the two-by-four-bay space into four openings per bay. I hung a translucent, shimmering cloudlike material behind these openings to screen the windows.

To represent humanity's Darwinian linkages, I suspended a timber roof of small trees, bracketed off the beams, within each bay. These three-inch-diameter sassafras trees were cut from the Michigan farm of Rich Brychta, who built Boardwalk, and were interlaced with rawhide straps. Into these eight bays were placed iconic Ethospace work stations. Carol Naughton then accessorized the stations with various primitive artifacts to symbolize the unity of form and function through time.

Since visitors had to proceed through the main portion of the showroom to reach this display in the rear, I designed a transitional room of concrete block with a painted trompe l'oeil mosaic floor patterned after one I had found and photographed in the ruins of Hadrian's first-century villa in Tivoli outside Rome when Stanley and I had explored it as residents at the American Academy. In front of the apsidal rear wall rested a "stone" wheel, emblematic of human invention. From this "reception room" one proceeded right into the audiovisual room, the walls of which were covered with panels upon which we "painted" cave drawings from Lascaux in France. Here the invitees were apprised of the nuts and bolts of the Ethospace system, and then they were escorted across the "reception room" and into the main exhibit to kick the tires of the actual product. The display was published in *Interiors* magazine in May 1985.

Our next assignment was to redesign the entire showroom for Neocon '85. The exhibit, in only one-quarter of the showroom, opened in the fall; by the following spring the other three-quarters was to be completed. With that timeline before us there was no time for equivocation either on our part or on Herman Miller's. I proposed that the ordered post-and-lintel structural system that formed the basis of our original exhibit be extended into the other three quarters but that in each quadrant the building materials change to express the historic range of architectural construction. The showroom entrance quadrant was composed of corbeled brick. On the left was a quadrant of strapped heavy timber and, on the right, a quadrant of bolted steel panels supporting steel I-beams. Into these measured series of bays I worked with the facilities design group to place an extended display of Ethospace, which was organized as a typical office system. To showcase the flexibility of the product, we conceived of a Mondrianesque primary color palette for the tiles set into a black frame. These fabric tiles would alternate with a black-and-white series and every night during Neocon the tiles would be changed, so that a new color scheme would appear each morning.

For this piece of artistry we won a product display award in a competition juried by *Interiors* magazine and the Chicago chapter of the AIA. The next year I again worked with the group in Zeeland, Michigan, on another variation of the Ethospace theme. For 1986 we replaced the tree-grid ceiling in the rear with open web joists. This three-year association concluded with an award from the local AIA chapter. The showroom itself survived for several more years until Herman Miller relocated to another floor with higher ceilings.

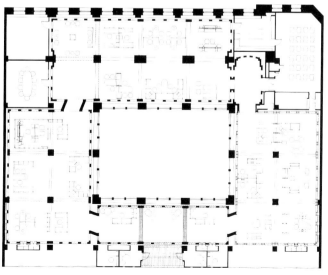

0 5 10   20 ft

WIT'S END:
THE GLASS HOUSE

Sawyer, Michigan
1985–87

The first two years that Stanley and I lived in Boardwalk we were befriended by certain local residents who were not offended by our corrugated-metal box. Neighbors Jack and Elaine Williams, who owned the nineteenth-century Centennial Farm that abutted our western flank, enjoyed the juxtaposition of our two properties. But others had complained about it sufficiently to cause the township officials to amend the zoning ordinance to exclude the use of industrial materials on residential buildings in Chikaming Township. Fortunately we fell in with other expatriates. I learned much about horticulture from a Dutch man named Teo Grootendorst who owned a nursery that provided us with indigenous trees and shrubs. Stanley spent Sunday mornings sitting around the pickle barrel at a deli owned by former mayor Jane Byrne's chief of staff, catching up on town politics with Bob Zonka, the editor of the *New Buffalo Times,* who was the former city desk editor of the *Chicago Daily News.* The fourth estate had discovered Harbor Country long before we did.

But soon other Chicago friends began to migrate to the area. One of the first was Rhona Hoffman, an art-gallery owner. For several summers she rented a frame cottage that perched on a sand dune overlooking the lake in the neighboring town of Sawyer. To that aerie came a collection of art historians and collectors. Many Saturday evenings we gathered on her deck for conversation; one of many friendships that grew out of those Bloomsburgian weekends was with the graphic designer Michael Glass and his partner, Bryan Fuermann, a Quixotic insurance executive with a Ph.D. in Victorian literature. They decided to build a home of their own.

Their property search turned up a sandy, level plot in Sawyer at the end of a washboard gravel road. It was located just behind the high primary dunes that form the eastern shore of the lake, and it fit their criteria of a secluded sunlit site where Michael could organize planting beds on its four acres and Bryan could read in solitude. They became my first from-scratch house clients. I had just completed the remodeling of an old clapboard cottage in the adjoining town of Harbert for another couple from the Bloomsburg circle and was starting on yet another in Harbert Woods for an artist.

To our first official meeting in the summer of 1985 Michael and Bryan brought a book filled with illustrations of planter homes of the Federalist period built along the Natchez Trace, a region they had visited earlier that spring. As we leafed through a hundred pages of substantially sized antebellum homes they were quick to point out, with a wink, that while their project was to embody the essence of that earlier era of perceived gentility and grace, this embodiment had to be accomplished parsimoniously. We discussed the feelings of solid comfort that friends' Connecticut houses of the 1920s seemed to personify, with their casual rooms filled with the light that flowed through french doors and across flagstone terraces. We talked about guests. They anticipated extended stays by friends and also contemplated possibly renting out two bedrooms to other friends to defray the mortgage costs. And so with this program in mind I embarked on the design of a three-bedroom house that atypically would locate two guest bedrooms on the ground floor and the master bedroom above. My own house slept eight in eight hundred square feet, less the silo; my clients allowed me double that amount to accomplish their desires.

I quickly determined that the most space- and cost-efficient plan was a slightly expanded version of Boardwalk, a central piazza flanked by sleeping quarters at one end and

cooking/bathing quarters at the other. The rectangle became cruciate with the addition of the colonnaded trellis and columned screened porch that abutted the internal court at front and rear. Above the large screened porch we planned an upper deck that opened off their bedroom, a lookout over the croquet court and a retreat when guests occupied the lower quarters. The spatial challenge then became that of locating the stair to the second floor. The only space that was underutilized was the kitchen, since the formal composition of the plan decreed a symmetrical disposition of elements about the center. And so the servant stair of a Federalist home became the master stair. This unorthodox staircase allowed for late-night foraging and became a favorite seat for conversations with Michael and Bryan during their gourmet cooking sprees. The double-height space also served to

draw the heat from the stove upward and out the clerestory windows.

The budget reared its head again to determine that doors would be a standard six foot eight inches tall and ceilings a normal height. But how to achieve the stateliness of its antecedents in this miniature version? Here the Prairie school master Frank Lloyd Wright's spatial conventions superimposed themselves on the scheme. A three-foot-deep soffit that ringed the living room lowered the ceiling to seven feet, causing the doors and windows to appear to be a sumptuous full height. This compression of space reversed itself in the room as the ceiling stepped up to a seemingly grand nine feet, replete with ceiling fans. The soffit also carried return-air ductwork and concealed the underside of the stair ascending to the master suite and descending again to its bath tucked above the guest rooms.

Important budget splurges were those that were instrumental in imparting verisimilitude and value to the building: the standing-seam galvanized-metal roof used only industrially in the Midwest but so much a part of Southern tradition; true divided light windows, each pane its own entity as in the past; and cedar clapboard lapped with the minimum exposure, to maintain the maximum effect of light and shadow and scale. We toyed with cheaper solutions (asphalt shingles, vinyl siding, snap-in muntins) but Michael and Bryan always found ways to save in certain areas so as to spend on the essentials. Our scrounging sensibilities matched so well that the search for interesting inexpensive fixtures and materials was fun. But as we closed in on the budget, and on a contractor selection for "Wit's End," as the project had fondly become known, it occurred to

Michael that the house was missing a storage shed for bicycles and garden implements. In our constricted square footage we were also shy on the niceties of covered entry and mudroom. And so the shed attached itself to the house by means of a breezeway off the kitchen, thereby solving this deficiency as well. But this new appendage unbalanced our carefully composed symmetrical plan, and so I sketched a solution, a columned screened porch at the opposite end adjoining the guest rooms, with a roof and footprint matching those of the shed. This would be the private domain of guests, and it did indeed become a most sought-after summer retreat, with its beaded-board ceiling and slow-moving fan. The paired additions strengthened the scheme since the gabled rooflines stepped down a second time from the center gable. Within a total of 2,300 square feet we had created a structure that appeared to be many times that size when the house was published in *Architectural Digest* the spring after my clients moved in. Joseph Giovannini, the author of the article, quoted Bryan: "She's the Jane Austen of architects. She can create a small world out of a small place, a microcosm in a two-inch piece of ivory."

Over the ensuing years I have watched their garden grow as the accouterments of an English landscape were added to the grounds: first the seven-foot white rhododendrons scattered along the edge of the woods, then the mounds of hydrangeas close to the house, and finally bed after bed of perennials. I designed a fence to enclose the gardens and a trellis to shade afternoon tea drinkers and croquet players.

Michael died in June of 1994 after a long illness. His memorial service was held on wooden folding chairs lining the empty croquet court. Bryan sold Wit's End in 1998 and moved to Boston to study landscape history at Harvard's Graduate School of Design.

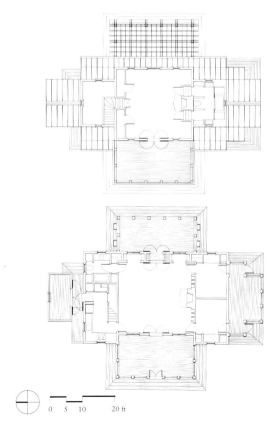

0   5   10   20 ft

COULTON POND RANCH

Clark, Colorado
1986–89

My memories of designing this ranch house correspond to the school year of 1986–87. It was during this time that I spent two semesters as a Loeb Fellow at the Harvard Graduate School of Design. For three days at mid-week I stayed in Cambridge, which meant that Chicago clients were relegated to the beginning or end of the week.

This fate befell my Suhu Gallery client, who chose that year to commission a log house in Clark, Colorado, some twenty-odd miles from Steamboat Springs. For years he had spent summer vacations with his family on a dude ranch in the Elk River Valley, and the owner of the property had just

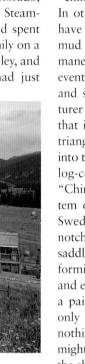

agreed to sell him a thirty-five-acre parcel at the entrance to the ranch. The site abutted the Routt National Forest and looked down the valley toward Buck and Flat Top Mountains and Ute Pass over the Continental Divide. His dream was to spend summers on the ranch when the art market was slow but also to set up a print-making facility in the valley, along with an artist-in-residence program to produce revenue during that off-season. He brought me out to the ranch after Labor Day to see the acreage and to talk to some local builders.

I had been working with this client off and on for ten years and thought I knew his personality and predilections

pretty well. What he wanted was the kind of authentic log construction that comes in children's Lincoln Log kits—in other words, the same round log is on the inside of the house that is on the outside, and the logs, with notched ends, are stacked on top of each other alternating with their perpendicular counterparts to form the four walls of a simple cabin. Because by nature the logs are uneven, there is a crack or "chink" between them that is "chinked," or stuffed with insulation. In other centuries this material could have been moss or a combination of mud and grasses. These were impermanent solutions, since the materials eventually dried and crumbled away, and so a twentieth-century manufacturer invented a plasticized material that is spread with a glue gun over a triangular wedge of styrofoam stuffed into the chinks. Naturally enough, this log-construction system is called "Chinking." But the most prized system of log construction is called the Swedish cope. Each log is hand notched on its underside to fit like a saddle over the log below, thereby forming a tight fit between the logs and eliminating the need to chink. It is a painstaking process that is selected only by those aficionados who think nothing of a building process that might stretch over several years, given the shortness of the building season in alpine regions. We were intrigued by the Swedish cope but knew that the timeline achievable by Chinking was far more realistic.

However, the ranch buildings were constructed using a third system, called the D Log. This is the most expedient system and uses a smaller, more readily available log that is thermally less effective. It is also milled into a D shape. Three sides are square and the fourth is left round and bark-covered. The square sides, as in the hand-hewn square-log houses built in the eastern half of the country, fit more tightly together. However, the D Log construction is only a structural frame and requires that a secondary

municate with his three children from any place in the house. This desire suggested an open plan above as well as below, and so the living room, with a river-rock fireplace, became ringed by a balcony on three sides that was reached by a double staircase. Clerestory windows would bring needed light into the room below. We planned for the kitchen to open directly into this room, separated from it only by a ten-foot-long cooking island replete with an industrial stove and many other commercial accouterments. An adjacent cast-iron stove beckoned family to gather about it. Bracketing this room would be a large pantry and dining room. To complete the ground-floor program the client wanted an office and a den/guest bedroom with a bathroom that would also service a spa on the opposite side of the living room. To this he added a large mudroom across the back, as well as a wrap-around porch. Upstairs two children's bedrooms, each with a bath, opened off the upper balcony, as did the master suite, warmed by a wood-burning stove, across the way on the opposite side.

We continually tallied the square footages. My client was shooting for a number of dollars per square foot times four thousand square feet, but the program exceeded this, and later, when he married his second wife, the program expanded a bit further through the addition of a banquetted breakfast room. However, he optimistically instructed us to prepare a preliminary set of bid documents based on the dream scheme, which we did. He decided, for the time being, that we should specify D Log construction. The following spring we issued the drawings for preliminary bids to a list of contractors compiled by his own research and interviews. He selected the bidder in the middle, an émigré from southern Illinois who agreed to a time-and-materials contract, which my client

wall be erected on the interior, behind which insulation can be placed. The D Log, besides being of a diminutive scale, also looks inauthentic when the logs are exposed on the corners in their hermaphrodite state of half-round, half-square.

Unfortunately, we learned that all the old-time D Log builders had left the valley. My client agonized over building a house that did not match the ranch buildings versus selecting one of the other, more attractive systems that no one in the valley seemed able to build. He decided to defer the selection process until we had developed schematic drawings. We selected the site for the house. It was near an

aspen grove on a rise above the sagebrush meadow and would face down the valley. He contracted for the road to be built to the site using gravel from a creek bed on the property, thereby carving out a future fishing pond named Coulton, after the creek.

Back in Chicago we worked to formulate a plan that would compact the most into the least square footage. This meant, as it did in Wit's End, that rooms needed to be simultaneously rooms and corridors to other rooms. Thus the centrally located living-room scheme seemed appropriate. A divorcé, my client was a gourmet cook who liked to feel that at any time he could com-

was convinced would result in a more reasonable price.

While he was debating whether or not to reduce the size of the house to conform to his original budget, and contemplating what amenities to do without, I visited Mesa Verde with the Committee on Design. There I learned from an Aspen architect of Alpine Log Homes, a log-house company in Victor, Montana, that worked with an architect's plans, prepared shop drawings, selected ten-inch-diameter-plus standing dead lodge-pole pines from local forests, assembled the house in Victor, numbered every log, disassembled the house, loaded the logs on trucks, and shipped them to the destination, along with a supervisor to instruct a local construction crew in how to reassemble the house in less than two weeks. This company seemed to be the answer to eliminating the D Log, and so I sent them our plans for an estimate.

The price for the logs came back; when we multiplied it by three, as advised by the log company, it seemed we would net a satisfactory house. We consulted with the contractor who, although he had never built a log house before, was confident that he could. He reviewed his numbers and concurred with the estimate. My client decided to proceed and, as we suggested, hired a local engineer to prepare foundation drawings, because the soil borings indicated expansive soils. There were many construction details and material selections yet to be hammered out, but it was late summer and the all-too-short building season was coming to a close. So the log-kit order was placed with Alpine Log Homes.

After several months passed, the foundation was poured and ready and the kit was assembled in Montana. It was late October and erection time was running out when the local building department took exception to Alpine Log Homes' structural construction details. We had decided to support the two-story living room with a ridge

beam and purlins bearing on two elegantly bowed fur trusses with wrought-iron tie rods, which in turn bore on the log structure. Alpine Homes' structural engineers had determined that the Montana logs could bear the weight of the roof and had proceeded to produce the house based on that premise. The Colorado Building Department disagreed. To resolve the impasse our local engineer designed a system whereby a steel column was inserted in the wall between the windows at the bearing point of the two trusses and then additional steel shims were inserted between each log that fanned outward from underneath the column to distribute the load across the

face of the structure. Once that crisis was resolved, the house was indeed assembled in nine working days.

It was by then late November and winter had arrived. I had arranged to meet my client at the site just after the new year of 1988. When the owner and I first approached the building, it stood mute in a windowless, roofless state awaiting the chain saws that would cut the openings and bring light and liveliness to the facade. We stood inside the house knee-deep in snow and gazed up at the blue sky and at the contractor standing on a second-story scaffold, and we were awed by the massive size of the logs. We knew then that the interior millwork and detailing would

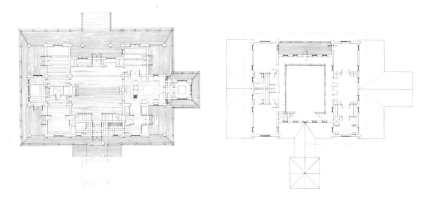

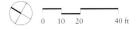

0   10   20   40 ft

need to be of an appropriately grand scale. But the initial charge was to roof the house to secure it from the weather. Then, as knowledgeable log builders will advise, the house should sit for a year to allow the weight of the roof to completely compress the logs to avoid continuous wall settlement after the interior is complete.

The work proceeded, but as is true in many communities with spectacular natural resources and recreational areas, many tradespeople partake of those amenities first, relegating work to a position of secondary importance. Workers appeared and disappeared as the fishing and hunting seasons waxed and waned, and the building process slipped further and further behind the schedule my client had set. At the same time he added more details to the house, including whitewashing the logs throughout the interior to brighten the rooms and using a rabbited buck detail at the window and door openings; we designed it to permit the use of casings on irregular log walls. This shadow box worked perfectly, but each opening required many hours of labor to perfect. The meter was also running on the hourly time-and-materials contract that my client had signed with the contractor, and we were rapidly learning that multiplying the log costs by three, or even four, was not the answer. But once committed to a house that embodies every desire, it is almost impossible to relinquish any part of the dream. In the end the house cost no more than others with the same number of amenities and details and level of finishes, but it was not a bargain either. Eventually the client took occupancy of the house in the winter that concluded with the spring fire that destroyed his Chicago gallery. I worked on the house for another year, completing exterior details such as railings, decking, and wooden gutters and all of the interior design while simultaneously attempting to re-create for him, in a rapidly declining art market, a smaller storefront space with some semblance of the spirit that prevailed in his original gallery.

CAMP MADRON

Madron Lake, Michigan
1987

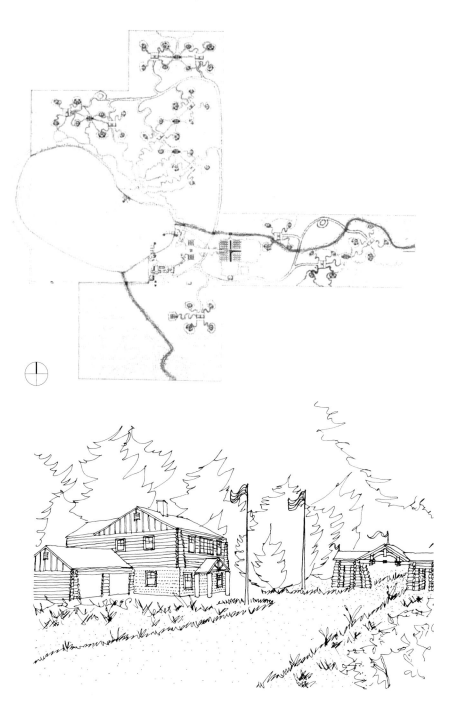

During the summer of 1987, when I was immersed in the translation of the Coulton Pond Ranch from a D Log to a chinked-log construction system, a Chicago developer announced a closed competition to adapt a former Boy Scout camp in southwestern Michigan into saleable vacation house sites, complete with comfortable cabins and a clubhouse. We were one of five invited firms. The remuneration was minuscule, but the developer arranged for the drawings to be shown in a local gallery, and so, in a competitive spirit, we all capitulated. The brief required that a site plan be developed, that suggestions be made for recycling the old camp buildings, and that concepts for a new series of cabins be conveyed. These were to be buildable, practical constructions that would compel potential buyers (mainly Chicagoans) to remember Midwestern summer camps they had known and loved.

I drove over to scout the area one sultry Saturday in August, and with every mile I drove away from the lake the temperature seemed to rise a corresponding degree. When I arrived at the overgrown campsite beside Lake Madron and saw the abandoned log-sided main lodge, I thought immediately of designing a new camp composed of real Montana logs. I completed my circuit of the site and returned to my drawing board in my loft at Boardwalk to begin to design a system of log cabins that would convince the builder to award us the commission. The schemes were for charming but cheap cabins clustered in woodland circles or along the lakeshore. (This was during the months when I was still multiplying the cost of an Alpine Log Homes kit by three.) I put the Coulton Pond team back together, and we worked diligently for a month to develop pen-and-ink drawings of these dwellings, as well as a detailed site plan. A three-by-four-foot drawing centered the site plan, which was bracketed by perspective vignettes of the camp that transformed it into a year-round permanent playground. I described it in my entry brief as follows:

Formerly a Boy Scout camp, this three-hundred-acre parcel in rural Michigan is now intended for development into forty-four country home sites. To preserve the memory of the camp, the cabins are clustered in eleven encampments nestled in the woods. Each four-cabin camp shares parking facilities. The camps might have names such as Webelo, Arrow, or Eagle. The existing lodge and caretaker's cabin will be remodeled and will serve as the base camp for recreational activities. The lodge is flanked by a pool pavilion that echoes its form and encloses a lap pool. A picnic pavilion engages the pool pavilion for outdoor barbecues. The primary beach and playground area is encircled by a boardwalk that connects the lodge, pool, and picnic pavilions with the boathouses at the water's edge that end in belvederes. Inside the grassed ring, games of croquet, boules, and bocce ball are played. In winter, this area is flooded for skating, hockey, and curling. Tennis and paddleball courts flank the boardwalk and establish an axis that is crisscrossed with a path that meanders up through the fruit orchard to the lookout tower. On the cross axis from the tower, grape-arbor pergolas lead to a footbridge on the north, the playing fields to the south, and the archery range to the east. From this summit trails wander farther east through the property to the wildflower meadow and communal gardens at the easternmost edge. Within the meadow martin houses attract birds in the summer and salt licks entice wildlife in the winter. The property is laced with summer hiking trails that convert to cross-country ski trails in the winter. These trails connect informal nature spots with more formal activity areas and create an interesting interplay of human-made and natural environments.

I then proceeded to analyze all of the existing structures and to propose alternatives:

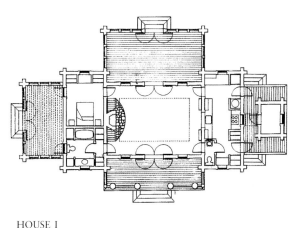

HOUSE I

The caretaker's house located at the front entrance automatically becomes the flagship building for the camp and as such should be upgraded. Log siding should be extended to the ground floor or stone facing applied, an attractive entry designed, a garage added on the west, windows balanced and framed, and the electrical service concealed.

The main lodge is intrinsically an attractive structure, although several awkward additions to the south and east partially obscure its character. The shed on the south should be removed or reconfigured. The shed roof over the entrance should be revised to a pitched roof and the window proportions changed and frames added. The building should be modified to open onto a deck on the lake side to take advantage of views. This can be simply done by adding entrances off the dining room and old staff rooms onto the deck. The interior needs restoration and the extent of the renovation is dependent upon a decision as to the winterization of the structure and its future use.

The existing boathouse is a ramshackle structure not in character with the lodge and should be replaced. The swimming pools should be razed. Assorted other small buildings could be relocated about the site to serve as tennis shacks or equipment storage.

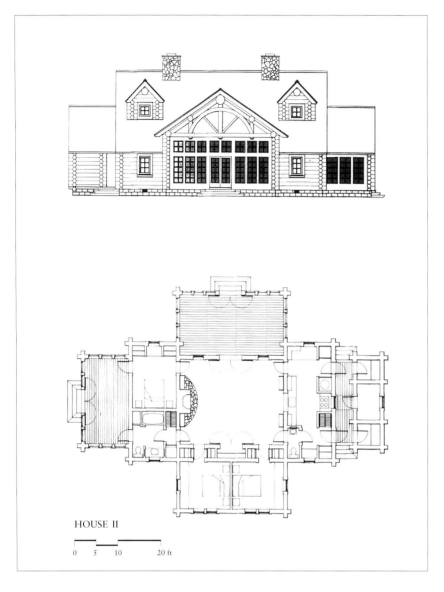

HOUSE II

```
0    5    10        20 ft
```

The hill house should be repaired and used as a guest house to provide prospective buyers with an opportunity to savor the pleasures of life at Camp Madron.

Last, I described the basis of the log-construction system for the new cabins, pointing out its benefits and those of the plans, which expanded incrementally from a common core, not unlike the centralized communal living space of Wit's End and Coulton Pond Ranch:

All "cabins" are designed using a ten-inch-round seasoned lodgepole pine log as the structural system. Houses will be erected, saddle-notched from a custom log kit provided by a Western log-home builder who supplies engineered shop drawings and a representative on the site during assembly as part of the package. Houses can be erected within a one-week time frame. Window and door openings are cut in after assembly. The preferred system would be a log-roof structure with cedar shakes although a conventional roof can be built with potential cost savings. The log mass is sufficient to provide appropriate insulation as well as a durable and attractive interior finish. The intent is to consider painted windows and doors with color options of "barn red," "lake blue," "forest green," or "stone gray." French doors function as windows to extend axial vistas.

All houses have pitched roofs and dormers for light. Ceilings are a minimum of ten feet to permit fans in all rooms to counteract the dog days of summer and to provide recirculation of warm air in winter. Plumbing stacks will be routed up through chimneys to avoid unsightly flues. All houses have provisions for stack washer/dryers since this convenience becomes a necessity in isolated areas, and all houses have bookcases (another necessity for erudite Chicagoans). Fireplaces are faced with flagstone to extend the rustic vocabulary, but box and flue are conventional prefab units.

Most kitchens have pass-through

communication with a "great room" but are semi-discrete from it, based on the theory that neither is a Hot Point refrigerator a work of art nor does a modern stove evoke the same nostalgia as its wood-burning predecessor. Rear mudrooms with adjacent toilet and closet adjoin the kitchens for practical purposes and thus free the great-room main entrance for expansive views into the forest.

The great room and main porch are identical in all houses. These rooms are calculated at sizes appropriate to function. Life in the summer revolves around the porch and one sized for both dining and lounging seems appropriate to all owners. In fact, all houses are modules of each other using the base of House I. The addition of two bedrooms identical in overall size to either wing of House I transforms it automatically into House II. If the loft options above each wing in House II are taken plus the loft option in House IA (converted to a family room) that house could become House III. The addition of the loft option in House IA to House I or IA converts it into House II plus and so on. The permutations are endless. In fact, all the wings are interchangeable or reversible so that the houses can be oriented to site and solar conditions.

In spite of all my efforts to entice the developer to select our schemes, he must have decided that three times the log costs was inaccurate arithmetic, because he chose a competitor's stick-built solution. However, when I stopped to inspect the property a year later I discovered that my site plan had been put to use rather than the competition winner's. The lodge was renovated and a few cabins built and sold. However, a few short seasons later Camp Madron vanished from the realtor's listings. Apparently it was the last unsuccessful domino to fall in a precarious stack the developer had set up, and he filed for bankruptcy as the 1980s came to a crashing close.

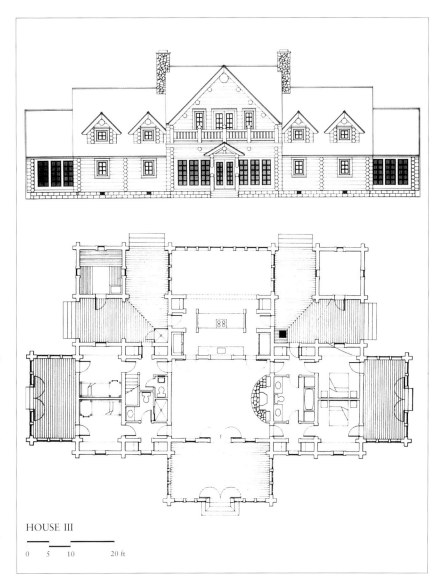

HOUSE III

0   5   10   20 ft

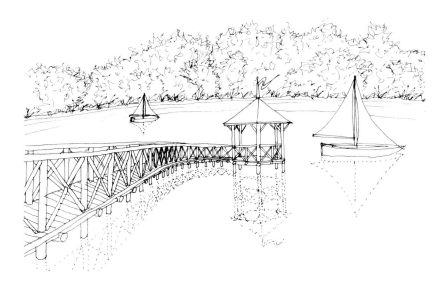

51

HAWORTH

Chicago, Illinois
1988–90; 1992

About a year after I had completed designing artful Ethospace systems in Herman Miller's Merchandise Mart showroom, one of their top competitors, Haworth, approached me to do the same for their product, Places. Haworth's partition system had neither the dimensionality of Herman Miller's nor the versatility of modular tiles, but it did have glazed panels with different snap-in muntin packages and oblique or pedimented tops, the shapes of which presented intriguing possibilities. My assignment was to create a front-window display to attract the Neocon audience of 1988. Since this window stretched for two hundred feet, I had a lot of space in which to let my imagination wander.

As I started to study Haworth's systems, I was struck by how closely their twelve-inch-wide Places partition with its pitched top resembled a picket fence. When I learned that it

was offered in a white finish, an idea began to form. What better way, I mused, to showcase a product than to use it in unexpected settings—to semitransform it, not beyond comprehension, but into an uncanny shock of recognition that would stretch the imaginations of those facility managers. Thus was born the "Hamptonian vignette," as we dubbed it, in which one imagines Dashiell Hammett sitting on his gabled front porch picking out a *Sam Spade* episode on his Remington portable. Occasionally he gazes out through his "classic" muntins into his garden, which is surrounded by a white picket fence and gateposts to reflect on the games strewn about on the "lawn."

Once my imagination was in action, it turned other gabled partitions into a medieval Gothic monastery with a resident monk ensconced at his desk in the scriptorium transcribing illuminated manu-

scripts. I thought the scene might remind Neoconites that not only did the company offer glass panels complete with a "Gothic" muntin kit but that the office itself offered opportunities for learning. The third, slightly more serious workplace was an extensively glazed conference room that doubled as a reading room. This unit utilized the "horizontal" muntin kit, while it showed potential users that conferences need not be conducted behind closed doors in windowless cubicles. That serious-minded Haworth would countenance such shenanigans was a tribute to their trust in my understanding of the architecture and design community, which appreciated the spoofs and awarded my concoctions a product display award.

The following year I was given the entire eight-thousand-square-foot showroom area for a stage set, with the proviso that I focus my attention

on the introduction of new fabric lines and colorways. Many of the colorations were intensely saturated, hues that reminded me of the Roman wall paintings Stanley and I had seen in Herculaneum. The year of 1989 was the pinnacle of the postmodern era. I also sensed that the recession was moving inexorably across the country, not unlike lava flowing down a mountainside. I therefore named the installation "The Last Days of Pompeii" and layered color upon color onto the office partitions, in combinations reminiscent of that doomed city.

That same year Los Angeles's Pacific Design Center decided to upstage Chicago's Neocon by holding a similar exposition, West Week, in the spring. So I was directed to turn my efforts toward energizing the Haworth showroom housed in Cesar Pelli's "blue whale." The showroom space occupied one of the sections of the whale's hump,

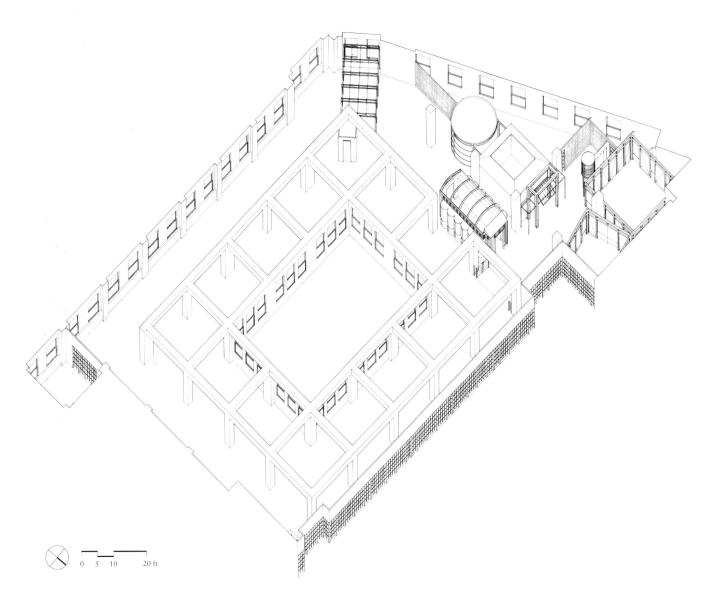

0 5 10   20 ft

and so my stage set sent King Kong in pursuit of Fay Wray up glazed office partitions that took the form of city skyscrapers. The message was clear. These muntinized panels were in effect miniature curtain walls that once connected would form individualized offices with windows. Thus employees placed in internalized work stations could enjoy the same perk as their executive counterparts who occupied external offices—the opportunity to watch the world go by.

I was also asked to remodel and refurnish one section of Haworth's corporate offices in Grand Rapids,

Michigan. The area selected was adjacent to the main reception room and would house one division of the corporation in newly configured work stations to showcase for visitors new product systems in actual use.

I was fortunate to be assigned to a young designer from Haworth who had a sense of humor. Gayle De Bruyn knew all the product lines so well that she produced the actual specifications, ordered product, and supervised the installations. We used to meet to confer on occasions at Boardwalk, which was the midpoint between our two offices. Sitting on the porch with a summer breeze

blowing across our plans we would plot surprises for the architecture and design community.

The third year of our association I was commissioned not only for the miniature offices but for the whole eleven-thousand-square-foot Merchandise Mart space. My charge was to create a showroom with an architectural blank slate that would be filled by the company's product. In other words, architecture was to take a back seat. I said that if architecture could move to the front seat in the third of the space that housed the support facilities and staff, I would create a background space in

the other two-thirds. We agreed and I proceeded in that larger display section to express the twenty-by-twenty-foot structural bay of the building in an orderly grid by cladding the concrete columns and beams in drywall painted white. I concealed the lighting, hung white mesh shades on the windows, and elevated the floor to run electrical conduit underneath. Mechanical and sprinkler systems followed the same simple grid set by the structure. The space became an abstract, styleless white box, except that it was separated from the "street" by a muntinized steel-and-glass curtain wall, also painted white. That wall grid recalled industrial construction and set the stage for a random assemblage of steel "outbuildings" that were superimposed against the grid. A fabric center, conference rooms, and a cafeteria were enclosed in forms that were designed to evoke images of the steel mills of Indiana that line the lakeshore and are seen from the Chicago Skyway, the symbolic southeast gateway to Chicago. These steel shapes became a metaphor for the entire steel industry, of which the office-furniture manufacturers form a major segment. In turn I had the fun of re-creating on a small scale some of those nostalgic forms that have fascinated me since childhood.

In 1992, I completed my last corporate work-station section in the home office. My stream of creative showroom displays had run its course. The sober 1990s were upon us and decisions were made to design Neocon displays in-house. Eventually, when its lease on the eighth floor expired, Haworth followed competitor Herman Miller down to the third floor, which had become the new mecca for systems manufacturers.

BRANDENBURG LAKE HOUSE

Fox Lake, Illinois
1988–89

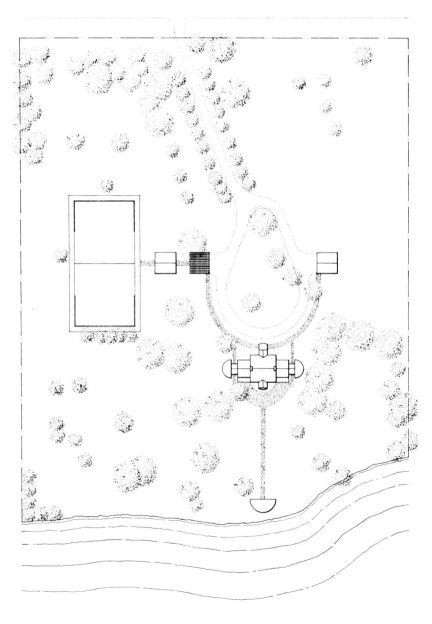

After Wit's End was published in April of 1988, I began to receive calls from previously unknown prospective clients. One of those calls came from a Japanese couple who had just purchased four acres of property on a tributary of Fox Lake, one of the "Chain o' Lakes" in the Kettle Moraine region along the Illinois-Wisconsin border. This land is dotted with interconnected finger lakes, left behind by the retreating glaciers of the last ice age, and is the source of the Fox River. It has remained a reasonably popular and accessible resort district for Chicagoans since the Milwaukee Railroad passes through the town of Fox Lake. When I was growing up in Beverly Hills, one of my best friends was a boy named Grant Pierce whose grandfather, a retired carpenter, owned a white clapboard cottage on the channel that connected Channel Lake with Lake Marie, two lakes in the Chain. Every summer I was invited to spend a week with Grant and his grandfather. We spent those days lazing on the grassy riverbank with one eye cocked on the bobber of our bamboo fishing poles or trolling in the Chris Craft on the connecting lakes in search of small-mouthed bass. I remember creeping out of the house at night with a flashlight to look for our bait, the night crawlers that surfaced when the dew was fresh. We never motored as far south as Fox Lake because Grass Lake sat between it and Lake Marie and that intermediary more than lived up to its name. It was a shallow lake choked with lily pads that constantly twined around propeller blades.

My clients' property was located at the south end of Fox Lake on a quiet inlet called Brandenburg Lake. When I drove up to inspect the site with them one autumn day, I realized that, although it was only fifty miles from Chicago, I hadn't returned to this part of the state for thirty-five years. Not much had changed. The small town at the edge of the lake was still shabby. At the local road-

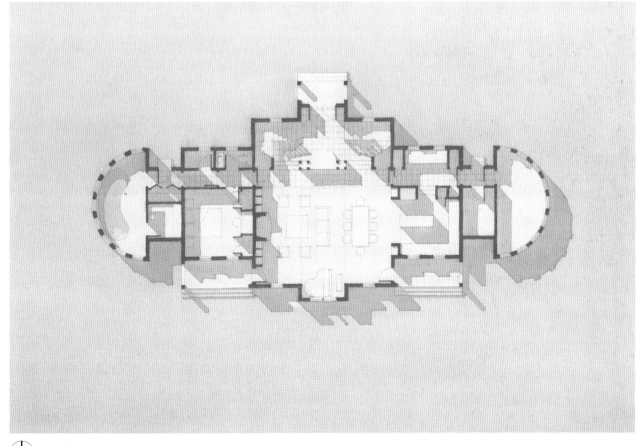

0   5   10   20 ft

house grass sprouted in cracks in the concrete parking lot, but the bait shop was still in business. However, it was an area whose time was about to come, as my astute clients had assessed. Already suburban sprawl had reached St. Charles, a charming old farming community on the Fox River fifty miles due west of Chicago, and it was rapidly spreading to the northwest along Route 12, the old two-lane highway that passed through the Chain o' Lakes on the way north from Chicago to Lake Geneva, Wisconsin. Strangely enough, Lake Geneva, which is three times the size of Fox Lake but another twenty miles farther northwest across the border, had all the cachet that the Illinois lakes lacked. The Wrigley Gum family built their summer estate on its shores, and the town itself sported an Italianate shopping and amusement arcade that stretched to the waterfront.

The house that came with the Brandenburg Lake property sat at the end of a spruce-lined allee that angled through the acreage, stopping before it reached the existing house, which sat on a corner of the site. It had a buff-colored flagstone base and a boxy board-and-batten top painted brown. A shed roof and twisted wrought-iron railings completed the picture of a modernist ugly duckling of 1950s vintage. Although I had hoped for my first contemporary commission, my clients had wanted a traditional Western house. In addition to being pretty and functional, the clients wished for this "American" house to incorporate certain principles of feng shui, the Chinese art of placement. The design process became one of the most fascinating and most difficult ones of my career. I tried to capture the essence of what they wanted (a collection of diverse American ancestors) without creating an incoherent building. We both had predilections for a certain orderly and formal relationship with nature that manifested

itself in my plans for their property.

The tree-lined drive directed traffic toward the far southeastern corner of the property where the old house crouched, so I decided to interrupt its course with a teardrop-shaped turnaround that would permit the new house to align itself at the broadest part of the drive on a north-south axis that paralleled the shore. I then sited the north-south tennis court, the tennis pavilion, and the trellised parking to the west off the center of the teardrop, with an opposing garage on the east axis. My plans repeated the formal axial disposition of the ancillary facilities inside the main house. A two-story foyer is flanked by a pair of winding staircases, only to be stopped by a columned case piece acting as the screen seen in Japanese temples, which is placed directly opposite the entrance to prevent evil spirits from passing through. Beyond and two steps below this object is a bridge on the east-west axis. The first-floor corridor beneath the bridge links the Japanese bathing pavilion to the west with the screened porch and pottery-making pavilion on the east. Both wings can be entered directly from the exterior so that tennis players can proceed directly to the changing rooms, shower, and spa, or family members into the mudroom and laundry. Feng shui decreed that for a child to remain unspoiled, his or her bedroom must be located in the southwest quadrant of the house; the son's room therefore abuts the bathing pavilion and shares a bath with this wing. Its symmetrical counterpart is the kitchen, which is located on the opposite side of the central "court." This center room is bisected from north to south by a gabled nine-foot-wide two-story space, which in turn is intersected by the bridge that connects the two second-story bedroom suites. The intended image is that of a medieval street, wherein the upper stories overhang and overlook the passageways below. The rear of the

house faces due south to the lakefront, where a boat-launching pavilion terminates the axis of the "street." To ensure an alcove for the grand piano and to express the arcade on the south facade, the two-story volume projects several feet farther in this direction. This projection caused a feng shui conundrum. Custom dictates that the southernmost part of a house should not have a window, and yet this projection puts the lake on axis and floods the interior with sunlight. My clients compromised, reasoning that since the house was located in a different hemisphere, a different interpretation of that compass point might apply.

Having determined that there was no builder within a twenty-mile radius of Fox Lake who had what we considered the necessary experience, we completed a set of detailed working drawings and sent the project out to bid to seven north suburban contractors. However, the end of the 1980s was still boom time in the house-building industry, and, citing other commitments, four of the seven contractors dropped off the list that they had agreed to be put on just weeks before. Of the three remaining ones, all of whose bids were high, a young builder from Barrington Hills, the most affluent of the northwest suburbs, seemed to be the most promising candidate. He did not appear to be frightened away by our complex set of bid documents, and agreed to work with us to reduce costs. But just as we began that process, my clients announced very suddenly but unequivocally in a meeting in the office that their plans had changed. They explained that they were very happy with the house as drawn and did not want to denigrate its design by changing details or altering materials. They preferred instead to stop the project. Some months later their mysterious departure was explained when we learned that they were preparing to move back to Japan.

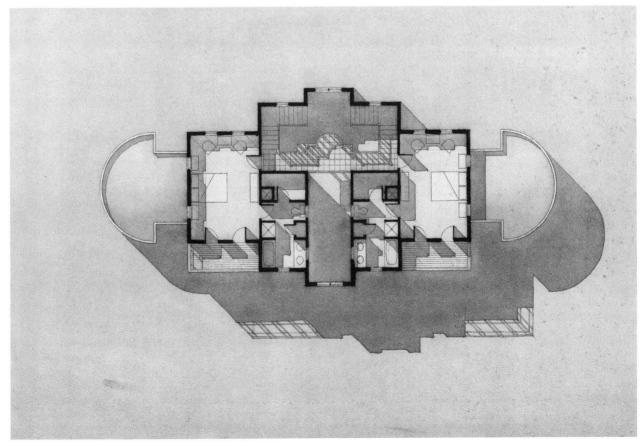

HILL ROAD HOUSE

Winnetka, Illinois
1988–98

One day in the fall of 1988, a prominent developer called our office to ask Stanley if he would be interested in discussing the remodeling of his circa-1929 North Shore residence. Stanley had been recommended to him by a partner in a construction-management firm with whom they both had associations. When the developer arrived for the consultation, Stanley immediately called me into the conference room. The drawing the developer produced of his house showed a blocky eight-thousand-square-foot limestone house with diagonally patterned lead windows and a Gothic arched entry. It was apparent that it had had an amalgam of English ancestors from differing centuries. It was part Jacobean, part Tudor, part Elizabethan, and more than a little Renaissance. We all sensed its need to focus on one parent. Either the stone parapet needed to be removed and a steeply pitched gabled roof needed to be added to the structure to reinforce the Gothic character, or the lattice windows and medieval doorway needed to be replaced. Other architects with whom the developer had discussed the project had suggested that the steep roof was the solution. We disagreed because we felt that the formal dispensation of rooms that was reflected in the rectangular facade placed it more solidly in the classical camp than the more romantic one personified by the Gothic revival. It was easier, we argued, to remove all traces of its Gothic roots, especially since certain additions were contemplated that would alter its character.

The discussion continued when we were invited out to inspect the premises, which we did on a cold and blustery afternoon in late October. The day stretched into the evening hours as we painstakingly analyzed room after room shivering in the chill the single-glazed windows could not overcome. What the developer was debating was whether the house was

worth restoring or renovating to the desired level of its progenitors or whether he should tear it down and begin all over again. The construction manager recommended the latter course, but in the end, since the client and his family had lived in the house for seven years and it had become home, and since the lot was one of the larger ones in this exclusive suburb, he decided to proceed with a remodeling and refurnishing plan. Little did any of us know then that this was the beginning of a process as well as a friendship that is still ongoing.

Hill Road House presented a rather serious site problem that had to be surmounted in order to expand it as the owners wished. The house faced south toward the street and was situated at the back edge of the property, encroaching far into the normal rear-yard setback required by the village zoning ordinance. The property was also located on a floodplain, and the village required that for any new

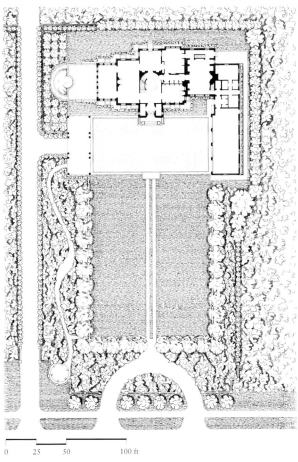

construction permits to be issued the owners had to build a retaining wall at the rear and slope the land to massive drains in the front yard. The clients were entering the property from the street along a drive paralleling the eastern boundary and driving into a two-car garage that was designated to become the family room. Thus they also wished to add a four-car garage and housekeeper's quarters onto the east side. We suggested these ancillary facilities should be placed perpendicular to the house, thereby creating a brick forecourt—a classical solution frequently used in European country houses.

We then persuaded our clients to relocate the existing driveway from the side of the property to the center and to build a semicircular brick entrance drive that would straighten out into a segment of two parallel tire tracks separated by a grassy strip that would be on axis with an extended front entrance. This driveway, when coupled with the building of a stone wall across the front, would screen the house from the street. The house was not completely centered on the site, but we extended symmetrical lengths of wall on either side of the two curb cuts as if it were and then stepped the extra western section back and inflected it around a stone *tempietto* that became the terminus of a woodland garden that absorbed the asymmetrical footage. We recommended a landscape architect whose work we admired, Maria Smithburg, who was trained at the Harvard Graduate School of Design. She designed all the plantings and the perennial gardens and consulted with us as we planned other site amenities. We kept the secondary entrance off the side lane for service vehicles but screened it with an arched wooden gate and a trellised arbor with stone columns through which traffic passed, driving over a grid of stone slabs set into the lawn. This vine-covered arbor began the path through the woodland garden on the southern axis and on the north opened onto a limestone-paved side court, which we extended to the west off the sunroom and wrapped in a stone balustrade. A circular fish pond and bubbling fountain continued this axis, along which Maria planted a formal grove of flowering crabapple trees that backed up to the twelve-foot-tall arbor vitae hedge that formed an evergreen wall along the western boundary. The evolution of the landscape was concurrent with that of the house, taking, all told, well over a year to plan and many more years to build.

The house itself was almost entirely gutted. However, we did adhere to the basic layout of the main rooms on the first floor, although each one was completely redetailed and the kitchen and rear corridor completely redone. The design and construction process became for those who worked on it an education. The level of research and study that went into re-creating

the interior was very high; we used the lessons of history to solve proportional issues of the present. Each room in the house had its own tale to tell, but there were certain design decisions that affected them all. First, the leaded lattice windows were replaced. Their single-glazed, unbraced construction caused them to flex inward in strong winds, and the air infiltration, as we felt it on that first cold fall day, was intense. After much agonizing and rejecting of all the mock-ups that attempted to create an authentic-looking leaded window that could be double-glazed, the owners decided to have the leaded windows specially built as single-glazed casements intermittently braced, which would unlatch with a lever and push outward, sliding along a steel rod. They also decided for the sake of authenticity to forego screens.

Our assignment had been from the start to re-create an interior that might have evolved gradually from

the original. Polished nickel was used for all hardware. In fact, we detailed the special knurled lever handles and escutcheon plates used on all the doors in the house based on a Jacques-Emile Ruhlmann design from the 1920s. This famous French designer was to play a most important role in setting a style for the house. Although antique Biedermeier became the owner's furniture of choice because of its exuberant lines and exotic wood veneers, we rapidly discovered that that period in nineteenth-century European history was devoid of any early lighting fixtures associated with it stylistically. However, the French art deco architects of the twentieth century had created sconces and pendant fixtures that transcended all styles in their elegance of line and proportion. To extend the authenticity of the house, the owners decided that no recessed ceiling lights were to be used, not even to accent the art. And so we began, while the house was under

construction and they were residing down the street in a rental house, to search auction houses and antique stores for period lighting of the 1910s and 1920s. Fortunately, the interior designer on our team succeeded in locating the finest fixtures by Ruhlmann and LeLeu and others of their ilk. When we could not find enough we made reproductions of the ones we could.

Although there were many rooms in the house, their proportions were not overly large by today's standards, and the ceiling height was just a comfortable nine feet six inches. To create the illusion of higher ceilings, we

designed crown moldings for each room that were shallow in height but deep in width, stepping up but mostly out from the juncture of the wall and ceiling in infinitely tiny increments, creating a myriad of shadow lines. New doors were also specially designed. Rather than using the existing french doors that were glazed to less than a foot from the floor, we had new ones made that were paneled below to a height that matched the window-sill height and were then transomed above to align with the rough openings for the windows already cut into the limestone facade. With this device we could maintain a more consistent propor-

tion between the doors and windows. The leaded-glass doors also extended vistas from one room to the next and into the landscape, to increase the feeling of expansiveness within the rooms. Each room was paneled in proportions that emphasized its height, thus reinforcing the illusion. All electrical and mechanical systems were also completely reengineered. Rather than concealing the air-supply and -return registers, we found a neoclassically patterned steel plate that we used everywhere, plating it in brushed nickel when used on the floors and centering it under windows and then painting it out when

used on the walls. The returns were also strategically placed and inset into the walls so as to minimize their profile. For each significant room in the house we built a ½-inch-scale study model, much like a dozen separate doll houses, so that we and the owners could visualize each proportional nuance.

The front entrance was tackled first. Its protruding profile was too shallow to hold many guests graciously in the outer chamber once they had stepped inside the raised-panel oak door. The doors to the closet and powder room also opened off the inner foyer, making entrances into the latter too conspicuous when

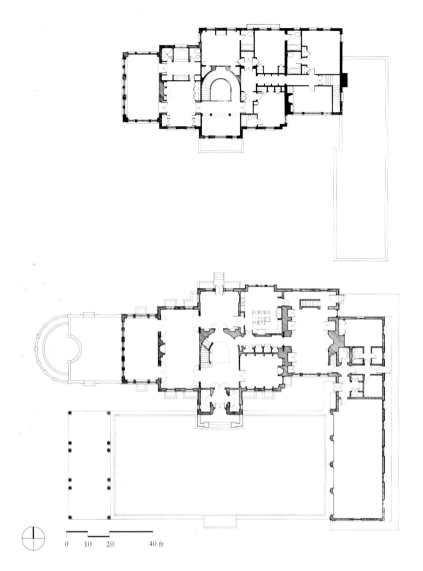

0   10   20   40 ft

many guests were assembled in the room. We corrected this by extending the entry out another six feet, thereby allowing us to detail a domed antechamber; doors to the closet and powder room could open off its octagonal form. This first-floor extension also created a balustraded balcony off the second-floor sitting room, which we created by removing the walls of an existing bedroom that had shut off light as well as space from the top of the staircase. Below, a pair of newly designed exterior french doors with a wrought-iron over-grid replaced their Gothic counterparts and flooded the entrance hall with light. Above those doors we commissioned a Chicago

sculptor, Walter Arnold, to carve a limestone overpanel that depicted two griffins bracketing the street address. He also carved several of the marble and limestone mantels. In the foyer we cut back the overhanging balcony on the second floor as far as possible to lessen the sensation of compressed space as one first enters this horseshoe-shaped room. The central skylight was raised up another two feet to increase the sensation of height as one ascends the stair; the railing was redesigned based on one in an eighteenth-century Parisian hotel. We chose a French limestone for the floor, which we had laid in a diagonal pattern accented by black marble inlays,

altering the scale and extending the proportions of the room. The antiqued gold-leaf statuary torchères were one of our first auction purchases. Gradually, over the past eleven years, appropriate antiques have been found for all the rooms, sometimes by us and sometimes by the owners in their travels. Carpets were woven abroad based on antique Savonneries or Aubussons or others we adapted and altered to suit our purposes. Semitransparent draperies soften the light. One of our French finds was the golden Ruhlmann pendant with silk shades hanging over our Ruhlmannesque table in the dining room.

The mantel in the living room was too large, and the fireplace protruded too far into the room because of the back-to-back flue it shared with its counterpart in the sunroom. We eliminated it in the sunroom, benefiting both rooms. Windows in the sunroom were replaced with french doors, and the fieldstone was plastered over to lighten the feeling of the room. The limestone floor reinforced that sensation as it extended out to the terrace beyond, and the missing fireplace permitted seating to be arranged against the wall facing out toward the courtyard and gardens. The wooden ceiling pattern with its silver-leaf insert was inspired by a yellow version I saw in a bedroom at Hvitträsk in Helsinki, Eliel Saarinen's Finnish home.

If the correct proportions could not be found in historical furnishings we created our own. Our dining-room table took its veneer cues from the Biedermeier chairs pulled up to it. The pair of doors into the ‚kitchen echo those from the living room, and the odd window in the west wall is balanced by an equally sized shallow cabinet across from it on the east. These devices order the room, as does the new paneling—the colored silk causes the walls to retreat, perceptually enlarging a relatively small room for the desired seating of fourteen.

We also added a french door on axis as one enters the room from the foyer to extend views into the rear yard.

The kitchen grew from gutting a butler's pantry and adding a two-foot-deep cantilevered bay window that became a banquette. All the cabinets were designed and the appliances selected to create the impression that the room had been unchanged since 1929. The library met a similar fate. An odd existing window beside the fireplace was balanced by a new mirrored one on the opposite side. The fireplace was reproportioned, a new black marble mantel and screen were designed, and new bird's-eye maple paneling replaced the Tudoresque oak. The simple herringbone pattern of the maple floors signified a private space, while the more public spaces sported appropriately scaled Parquet de Versailles patterns based on rooms in the Petit Trianon. Many of the moldings had the same basis as the flooring.

Even the basement was converted from a large unfinished utility room into a series of special rooms. These ranged from a wine cellar to a billiards room, and from an entertainment center to an exercise facility, in essence adding another floor of usable space to the complex. On the second floor, the ceiling in the master suite was raised and a parapet was added to the exterior facade. Three children's rooms with baths were carved out, as well as a guest room and home office, all reachable via a rear stair off the family room.

While the architecture is complete, the furnishings are slowly following suit as the correct pieces are found or invented. We proceed steadily, seeking to maintain the highest level of proportion and detail. It is a project to which some of our best designers have dedicated many years of service; in turn, Hill Road House has taught and trained them far beyond any ordinary design experience.

CHICAGO BAR ASSOCIATION

*Chicago, Illinois
1988–90*

Early on a Monday morning, December 12, 1988, Stanley and his son Judson left for Japan. Stanley's apartment building project in Fukuoka City on the south island of Kiushu was under construction, and he was due for a site conference. The same afternoon, our Hill Road House client, a developer, called to say that he had just been given the opportunity to submit a proposal to build a high-rise office complex for the Chicago Bar Association (CBA). However, a building scheme had to be presented to the governing board of the CBA by the following Monday morning. I told him that one-half of the team was en route to the Orient and would not return until that following Monday afternoon. Our client replied, "So you do it!"

He and his partner arrived in our office the next morning to present the particulars. Some work had been done by a previous developer and his architect, but it was immediately apparent that further efficiency and cost-effectiveness were called for. The site purchased by the CBA adjoined the John Marshall Law School building designed by Pond & Pond, and plans called for connecting to its sixth-floor library from the sixth floor in the new building. It was a small lot on the south side of the central business district that would yield floor plates of approximately six thousand square feet. The floor-area ratio permitted by the city zoning code for the property translated into a sixteen-story office tower of 115,000 square feet built flush to the lot lines. The previous scheme had produced a historicist red-brick building with Georgian overtones. Our developer decided that his building would shift centuries as well as materials and would be a limestone tower expressive of the linearity associated with the late-Gothic Perpendicular style, because a skyscraper should symbolize verticality. There was some precedence for the Gothic revival style in the

Loop, but aside from the eight-story University Club some blocks away on Michigan Avenue, the other examples were more ecclesiastic in character.

"How literally Gothic must this one be?" I inquired, hoping for some alternative. "How does a rose window sound?" he replied. Realizing that the first charge was to come up with a scheme that would convince the CBA to hire both of us, I crossed my fingers, figured that when Stanley returned we could together transport it into the twentieth century, and began to attack the problem on two fronts simultaneously. First, the module changed to one that was conducive to maximizing the number of standard-size offices that could be aligned across the front and rear facades, where the views were. The elevator and service-core location also changed to a central position, in order to present an orderly arrangement of offices around it as well. Second, a traditional facade needed to be adapted to a modern five-foot module, so that the fenestration made sense on both the exterior and interior. Once this problem was solved, the rose window appeared high above within the Gothic arched entry and centered itself in the CBA's formal meeting and dining room. Twin crenellated towers bracketed the small gabled edifice positioned atop the tall shaft. This double-gabled form took its clue from its Georgian predecessor, because the developer was concerned about deviating too far from a building type with which the board was already familiar. The team labored long on producing an intricate sepia watercolor drawing four feet tall for the presentation, and our client took to dropping by the office every evening on his way home from work to check on progress. He even appeared late on the Saturday night before our Monday deadline to offer encouragement and more variations on the Gothic theme.

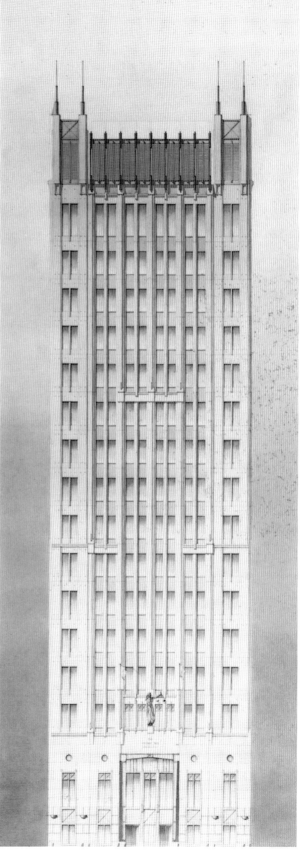

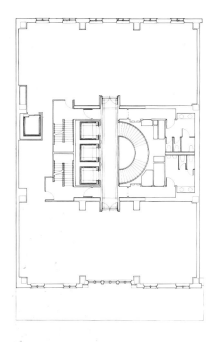

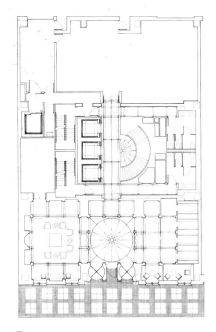

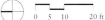

On Monday morning I presented the project as a contextual building responding not only to the well-known University Club by Holabird & Root but also to the nearby, Gothic-inspired Fisher Building by D. H. Burnham and Company. Although our building was far more literal, I also mentioned that Mies van der Rohe's Federal Center, only a block away, was actually an abstracted version of a neo-Gothic tower and had roots in the Perpendicular style, like ours. After a short deliberation on their part, I came away able to present Stanley, upon his return that afternoon, with our first office tower, albeit a traditional one. We thought this might be a temporary condition until we saw its picture in a press release the next morning and realized we were committed to some form of Gothic.

The building was to be in part a commercial condominium office building. The first seven stories would headquarter the CBA; the upper floors would house office condominiums that the developer would temporarily lease to other tenants until the CBA needed more space. In effect we had two co-owners and two clients to serve within a very short time span and with a very tight budget. We learned immediately that it was not only our scheme that had carried the day that Monday morning but the developer's promise to fast-track the project and complete the design and construction in less than nineteen months. We set to work in earnest with the construction-management firm whose partner had recommended us to the developer.

With time and costs of the essence, we looked for elemental building systems and simple construction solutions. We began to tackle costs by analyzing the structure. On close consideration, the five-foot module stood. It would be a poured-concrete post-and-beam three-bay structure with perimeter struc-

tural mullions ten feet on center. Granite would clad the building on its first three floors, stopping at a height corresponding to the cornice line of Binyon's Restaurant, its southern neighbor. The remainder of the floors would be clad in precast-concrete panels, which would be carefully matched to the color and texture of the granite. With the basics in place, we then campaigned to bring the facade into the twentieth century, where it could join other members of the Chicago school but still maintain its own identity.

The developer was completely supportive as we began the process. The first overly literal Gothic elements to be transformed were the arched and rose windows; the second, the gabled top, to be replaced by abstract steel louvers; and so on. While maintaining the corner towers, we substituted for the crenellations "stone" spires topped with sixteen steel pinnacles to increase the soaring quality of the slender tower. To reinforce this further, we began to subtly step the facade at three points to add definition and a sense of the shifting planes associated with more modern sensibilities. The first, most pronounced step occurs at the third floor and the second at the seventh to correspond with the cornice of the law school to the north. The third step was confined to the central shaft and occurs at the midpoint of the typical floors, but because its twenty-foot-wide section pushes up through the break at the seventh floor it reinforces the facade's verticality. In short, the building has all the attributes of a classical composition. A solid base of split-face rusticated granite gives way to a smoother, lighter texture as it rises, and then to the even lighter precast concrete of the shaft. Finally at the top is the lightest element of all—steel pinnacles reaching to the sky. There is a sense of medieval buttressing achieved by the more solid corners, but that is countered by the

building's efforts to resist gravity and to soar by lightening the material load as it ascends.

Maintaining the same fenestration pattern as the original scheme, our design became more abstract as we simplified the windows, tinting them and squaring them off in their anodized aluminum frames on the front and rear facades. Above the adjacent structures on the north and south facades, we shifted to steel-and-wire glass for the prescribed fire-code height. "Chicago Bar Association" was inscribed in granite above the revolving stainless-steel doors, and, in a gesture to his

To maintain its appearance in perpetuity, we selected an interior finish palette of durable materials—a terrazzo floor, a deep red-and-green Rosario marble wainscot (Mies van der Rohe's favorite), and mahogany and cherry paneling trimmed in stainless steel for protection. Our program for the first floor was ambitious. A concierge station was required to direct traffic, behind which were positioned coat racks. Other amenities included discreet phone rooms and, at the end of the hall, the first of many dining facilities. On the opposite side of the domed reception hall we designed

co-owners and potential clientele, the developer commissioned an interpretive aluminum casting of Themis, the mythological figure of law, to be positioned above the doors. We selected a local sculptor, Mary Block, to create this figure, which she suggested take the medieval form of a male holding in one hand a dove as the symbol of peace and in the other a globe signifying unity.

Our intentions for the lobby were to create a welcoming clublike atmosphere for the twenty-two thousand attorneys that might visit the headquarters at any given time.

an ample lounge with a wood-burning fireplace. Its stack rises sixteen stories in height, so there is always a roaring blaze to gather around on wintry afternoons. Across from the elevators and bronze doors engraved with mystical, hermetic symbols rises a circular terrazzo stair, clad in marble and silhouetted against a curved marble wall. This stair, with its deco-like steel railing, ascends to the large main reception hall and dining room. It was here in the fall of 1990, several months after its spring opening, that we celebrated Stanley's sixtieth birthday.

TIMBERLANE HOUSE

New Buffalo, Michigan
1989–90

At the end of the summer of 1989 I was hired by two businessmen to design a weekend home for them in Harbor Country. Stanley and I had just returned from Scandinavia. I had traveled to Helsinki with the AIA Committee on Design to lecture at an international conference on architecture and urban planning before catching the overnight ferry to Stockholm to connect with Stanley. We took a quick look at Gunnar Asplund's Woodland Chapel and Central Library before continuing on to Copenhagen. When we returned home and I accepted this latest commission, our office was running at full throttle and our staff was at full strength. None of us anticipated that exactly twelve months later the economic engine would run out of steam on its Chicago leg, and our office would begin to shrink like a slowly deflating balloon. In hindsight I see that this project seemed to run on a track parallel to that of the economy.

My clients were a lawyer and a banker who had purchased a piece of property on a bluff overlooking Lake Michigan in a newly developing subdivision named Timberlane. They had decided to exchange summer vacations cycling in France for year-round vacations in the sand dunes. As with much lakefront property in the area, the land was deeper than it was wide. We discussed issues of privacy, knowing that all residents would be allowed to build a single-story building within ten feet of the property line on lots that measured one hundred feet in width. Michigan's Department of Natural Resources, which controls land use along the shoreline, dictated that construction could only occur one hundred feet behind the ridge of the first dune, which when combined with the front-yard setback of New Buffalo Township left just enough land for the type of footprint I sought. My clients had asked for a house of approximately 2,500 square feet, in addition to a two-car garage.

They wanted two guest bedrooms and a master suite, a great room with an adjoining kitchen, and a screened porch. They stipulated that if possible all of the rooms should face the lake, as well as the woods in front. It was not possible to accomplish all this in a single story that was one room deep, nor was it possible in two stories, because the side-yard setbacks increased to twenty feet when a story was added. Two stories also still skimped on the room sizes they desired and spread the house out too close to the lot lines. I knew from a previous project that three stories were possible in the area if the lowest was depressed a foot; the midpoint of the roof of the highest was less than thirty feet high; and entry and egress occurred at the mid-level. I approached my clients with the thought of a third story that would allow all rooms to have a lake view and they were enthusiastic.

Since the two repaired to Europe whenever possible, I thought that the idea of a small-scale country estate might intrigue them, as indeed it did. I proceeded to create for them just such a complex in the tradition that originated in the Veneto with Andrea Palladio's design for the Villa Emo and emigrated to Virginia with Thomas Jefferson's plans for Monticello. Single-story carriage houses would flank the main three-story residence, forming a private forecourt that would be landscaped with parterre gardens in the European manner. The tripartite facade I designed mimicked an Italian Renaissance palazzo, in miniature. String courses divided the structure into base, piano nobile, and attic stories. The original scheme proposed cladding the base in limestone and the upper two stories in a synthetic form of stucco called Dryvit, but due to cost considerations clapboard siding indigenous to Michigan replaced the traditional Mediterranean stucco. Wider boards used at the ground level simulated the rusti-

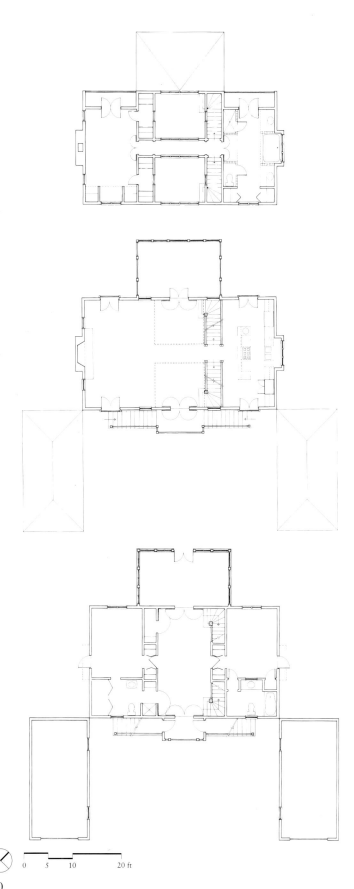

cation that the limestone would have provided while also expressing the weight of the structure. The guest quarters were to be located at this lower entry level. Pairs of stairs rising both internally and externally would lead to the public quarters on the principal floor, where pairs of transomed french doors opened onto small balconies and onto an upper deck above the screened porch on the lake side. The master suite was housed in the attic story, where sloped ceilings followed the hipped roofline. A bridge that spanned the double-height dining area below linked the master bedroom with its bath. Both rooms had the requested private recessed porches that would overlook the lake. While guest rooms on the ground floor would allow friends the freedom to roam outdoors, the upper balconies on the top floor would give the owners their own quiet retreat. The house's aspect was a dignified one, with a certain austerity brought about by the hierarchical order of the facades, symmetrical compositions that balanced classical components in the midsection with Midwestern variations on the top.

My clients were mature professionals who possessed the same quiet manner that I sought to portray in their house. No disagreements ever occurred between them in my presence. If it appeared that either one disagreed with any design issues, they would announce that the dispute would be settled before the next meeting and it always was. There was some question with reference to resale values in regard to my plan for paired semi-detached garages without direct entry into the residence in place of an attached two-car garage, but the two finally agreed that future purchasers might also appreciate that the uniqueness of the split garages lay in their diminutive scale, which increased the apparent size of the house. With this final hurdle to a coherent design

0   5   10   20 ft

surmounted, we finished the working drawings and sent the house out to bid in the spring of 1990. The clients had decreed that a complete set of specifications accompany the detailed construction drawings and that the bidding process be a formal one. Unfortunately, the bids were considered too high by my clients. As accurate forecasters of the impending recession they were in the process of considering whether or not to rebid the job in six months time when they were offered almost double the original price of the lot by a family that was anxious to snap up one of the few remaining unbuilt lake lots in the subdivision. My clients capitulated and sold them the property, along with my plans. And so, for the second summer in a row, a house whose construction I had anticipated was canceled before it was begun. A young draftsman in my firm, who by the luck of the draw had labored over an elaborate set of working drawings for both of the aborted houses, was so depressed after our second disappointment that he left the firm some months later. After several years I returned to the Timberlane site to discover that it was still an empty lot, and I wondered if the recession had caught up with its new owners, as it had with the rest of us.

UNIVERSITY CLUB

Chicago, Illinois
1989–91

In the spring of 1989, the House Committee of the University Club of Chicago interviewed us as one of several firms they were considering to remodel and refurbish their pre-function rooms on the second floor of their twelve-story neo-Gothic building on Michigan Avenue. I was especially interested in this Loop building because it had been one of the early prototypes for our Chicago Bar Association building designed the previous December, and I was intrigued by this particular set of rooms because it included the former women's dining room with its infamous rear stairs. My father had long been a member of the club, using its stately Cathedral Hall (a replica of Sir Thomas More's Crosby Hall) for special client lunches. The club was across Monroe Street from Schmidt, Garden & Erickson's offices, and when he wasn't hanging out with his cronies at the Cliff Dwellers down the street he was to be found in the lending library of the University Club. Every December, our family attended the club's annual Christmas party, held in the festively decorated Michigan Room. The tall limestone-framed stained-glass windows looked out over the avenue to the Chicago Yacht Club. This was the premier room on the piano nobile, if a Gothic building can be said to have one, and its ceiling by Frederic Bartlett was a prized attribute. This room was also the club's main breadwinner, rented out for numerous functions on an almost daily basis.

However, the adjoining room, the President's Bar, had none of the distinguishing architectural features of its neighbor. The location of the bar in this room also meant that it needed to be continuously available to all customers. Therefore, the club's board of directors was contemplating transferring the bar to what had been the women's dining room at the rear and renaming it the Monroe Room, instead of the West Room. I remem-

bered this room from occasional lunches with my father when I was working at SOM, and also remembered that I was required to enter through the ladies' entrance, located twenty feet down Monroe Street from the main entrance, and then to ascend to the women's dining room by way of the designated rear stairs. This inequity made me less inclined to dine at the club on any regular basis. But the dining experience was indeed an elegant one, carried on in an atmosphere of soft lighting from chandeliers and sconces, white linen tablecloths, and an accommodating staff. However, this setting was at some point in the 1970s transformed into a dark booth-lined space, suitable for the cocktail hour. This decor stopped my luncheon attendance entirely.

I was therefore curious to see its current configuration as I climbed the main staircase on my way to the interview room and paused at its doorway. The booths were gone, replaced by lounge seating reminiscent of SOM's corporate interiors. (I discovered later that the tuxedo sofas upholstered in red mohair were indeed remnants of that firm's involvement.) Admitting women to membership had finally removed the need for a separate dining facility, and it had become a members' reading room.

The initial assignment was to prepare a series of schematic studies of room usages and to attach a budget to them. Certain figures discussed by the committee appeared to be adequate not only to remodel the second floor but to wipe out all vestiges of the secondary quality of the second entrance. The goal of the board in a competitive marketplace was to encourage more members to hold more functions at the club and to create a more convivial environment in which to have them. My report included upgrading the cloakroom and elevator cab, as well as reconfiguring the stairs and removing the

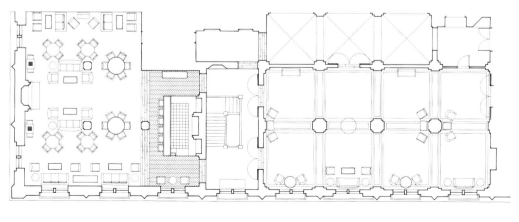

0 5 10   20 ft

travertine panels added to the entry in the SOM era. For the two primary rooms I proposed introducing or reestablishing traditional Tudor detailing. The form and detailing of the original English oak beams and Indiana limestone quoined columns in the main lobby and stair hall would be repeated in the former bar, soon to be the new lounge. The beams would serve a practical function as well as a decorative one by concealing the mechanical distribu-

tion system. Wood columns painted like limestone would be used in place of real limestone to protect the budget, and the room would open directly onto the main stair hall once the bar was removed from that location. The rear stair hall linking this room with the new bar room would become the President's Portrait Gallery. In the new bar room, the existing limestone fireplace strongly influenced the design of the new English oak bar, and we suggested painting the existing white trim and deco-

rative ceiling the same faux limestone color to shift it into the Tudor mainstream. By October I had completed several alternate studies requested by the committee after they had participated in reviews of our plans, and the schematics were released for pricing to a contractor.

I discovered after I was hired that I was not to be the architect of record, for a variety of reasons. Furthermore, although the House Committee had initially referred to monies available for the remodeling of the second floor in a range that

would have permitted substantial work, we later learned that the manager had earmarked a good portion of those funds for remedial work in other areas of the club. Late that fall the contractor submitted the pricing for our portion, which had included the remodeling of the first and second floors and new furnishings. We were paid for our feasibility study, and the project was put on hold until the following summer.

When we were recontacted in 1990, it was clear that the economy had tightened and the tenor of the committee had changed. One of the new members of the House Commit-

tee was James Nagle, who had worked for Stanley and with me, and he became the designated representative. Jim announced that the three-thousand-member club had decided to forego the more extensive renovations presented in our earlier schemes and to settle upon plans for the second floor that located the bar on the east wall of the former women's dining room. To minimize the disruption to the membership that the work would cause, it was decided that construction would commence at the beginning of the following summer and be completed by October first. All architectural materials and interior furnishings would be stockpiled in advance and warehoused, so that the work could proceed according to this tight construction schedule. We rushed to complete the initial architectural phase so that it could be priced and approved by the board of directors during their fall meeting. I made three separate design presentations to three successively more senior club organizations, beginning with the House Committee and ending with the full board of directors. Since our architectural presentations reinforced the Tudor character of the club, their only reservations were with my color palette, which proposed the use of intense, highly saturated hues for the walls of the various rooms. Jim's corroboration of the colors contributed to their acceptance. Indeed, the barn red of the new lounge became so popular that members of the Michigan Shores Club of Wilmette remembered the room when they were looking for an architect for their own remodeling a year later.

After we completed working drawings and the shop drawings were in progress, we tackled the furnishings and fixtures. The project was completed on time and under budget and won a local and national ASID Historic Preservation Award. However, still my greatest satisfaction is walking into the club through the front door.

THE LIGHTHOUSE

Martha's Vineyard,
Massachusetts
1991–93

Early in December of 1990 a Chicago couple called to talk to me about designing a vacation house for them on Martha's Vineyard. The call came at the precise moment when the long, dark winter days that foretold the deepening recession were beginning to lower my spirits, but the prospect of new work immediately lifted them again. In the office, the couple unfurled a site plan that showed a wooded acre of land adjacent to the coast. They began to discuss their dreams for this house, which might eventually become a partial retirement property for them.

I spent some time with the two of them, talking about how the house

might be sited and what type of character it might have and what homes on the Vineyard they admired and why. One of them belonged to an island contractor who had become a close friend and whom they intended to have build their own house. When the conversation ended and they were rolling up the plans and sketches in preparation for their departure, the husband mentioned that they also intended to interview local architects on the island and wondered if I could make some sketches that might indicate how well I had understood the kind of house they wanted. I responded that I would attempt to convince them of my capabilities to do that verbally rather than visually, that we needed to spend more

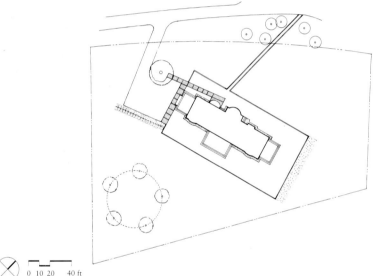

0 10 20   40 ft

time together, and that I needed to study the context of the island before I would presume to create the required image; and that meant that we needed to make a commitment to each other. After they left, I called their contractor on the Vineyard, as they had suggested, and he discussed with me the character of the part of the island where their lot was located and provided me as well with a profile of his friends. I was actually not that unfamiliar with coastal New England, having visited Nantucket as well as the Vineyard some years before, and so I composed a letter that I hoped would not only express the essence of an island home but would capture the spirit of that home:

The first-century Roman architect and engineer Vitruvius wrote in *De Architectura* that the fundamental principles of architecture are *firmitas* (durability), *utilitas* (convenience), and *venustas* (aesthetic pleasure). Certainly these three tenets seem to express your own concerns: that the house be well made and maintainable; that it be well planned and purposeful; and that it be well designed and deferential—not slavishly but sympathetically to the vernacular of the Vineyard.

The house should respect the island and yet establish its own persona—a personality that should reflect that of its owners. Its concerns

should be with comfort in all its forms—from convenience to commodity. It should be a restful retreat—a safe haven, a snug harbor. It should have spaces to assemble—accommodations for friends and family—and spaces to disassemble—nooks and crannies. Sand and wet bathing suits should not faze it. Breezes should blow through it, carrying the sound of bell buoys and the smell of salt air. Sunlight should cross its rooms in summer, and fires burn and crumble in its hearths in winter.

For all of its comfortable commodiousness it should be skillfully designed with modesty and prudence in mind. Enough time should be permitted in its planning for everyone to become comfortable with its design. The process from beginning to end should be stimulating and satisfying.

As the winter passed without further communication, my hopes dimmed, and by spring they had died. So I was completely surprised when they called at the end of the summer to say that they were prepared to sign a contract and to schedule a fall visit to the Vineyard. We spent several days together on the island touring houses the contractor had built (some by architect friends of mine) and recording on video our reactions to them. The inflected curves that Bill Rawn had used on his addition to a dwelling across from a lighthouse were noted, as was the unique window configuration and unusual scale of a Kliment and Halsband house on another part of the island. The nautical imagery of a modern widow's walk, fir cabinetry, and brass hardware in an Edward Larrabee Barnes cliff house were all registered on tape, as were several of the traditional homes in Edgartown. Before we left the island we had established an approximate size for the house—three thousand square feet—and outlined a program to fill it. The wish list included, from top to bottom: a widow's walk above the roofline; two second-floor children's bedrooms with play lofts and baths; two guest bedrooms; a

ground floor with a formal entrance; places to assemble, including a family room and kitchen and outdoor decks, one with a shower; and places to disassemble, a master suite and study. Last, at the bottom, a full basement with outdoor as well as indoor access was desired. All these rooms were to be combined in a house "whose simple lines would be graced by the right curves."

I returned to Chicago and set to work to transform the assorted images from different centuries into one coherent composition that would clearly represent its own century as it reinterpreted precedent in a singular way. In deference to those antecedents

from other centuries I ordered the house symmetrically and hierarchically, which created a formal presence that is reinforced by the grassy plinth surrounding it and removing it from nature. Our landscape architect, Michael van Valkenburgh, understood the house's need to exist in nature but to be separate from it, and his designs were a perfect complement, providing point and counterpoint.

Lest the house become too immersed in tradition, a playful lighthouse stair tower became the linchpin of the front facade. It spirals up to the widow's walk that surrounds the belvedere. The lowest windows of the lighthouse illuminate the basement

stair, which was tucked underneath the main stair so that children could run in from out-of-doors and descend directly. The tower also creates a stack effect, drawing warm air up and out of the un-air-conditioned interior. This Bernoulli principal of air movement fascinated my clients, who found it another clever link to the past. The inflected form of the stair tower is repeated on one end of the rear facade by the bow windows of the breakfast room and at the other end by the master bedroom seating alcove. The requisite curves also reappear in the trellis that animates this facade; its rhythm is echoed by the arched transom windows at either end of the house.

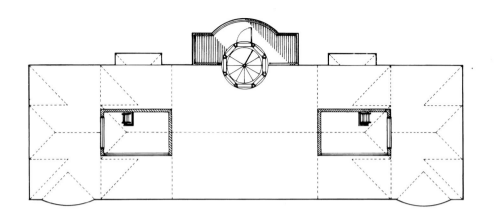

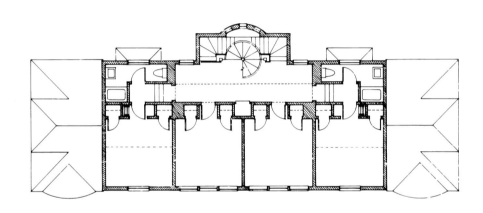

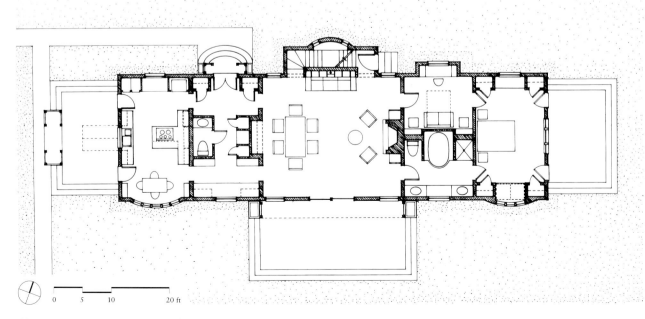

0   5   10   20 ft

The ground-floor rooms form an enfilade that progresses outward in twelve-foot increments from the twenty-four-foot family-room core. This central space steps up to allow for a ten-foot ceiling. Thus on the second floor one steps back down to the children's rooms at either end. Parallel axes transverse the house, permitting views into the woods from one end to the other through french doors. Windows aligned on the cross axis fill the rooms with sunlight and cross-breezes.

Ascending the tower to the second floor is the circular stair, which curls like a chambered nautilus up to the belvedere. Here on the second floor at the outboard sides each child has a mini-suite with an adjacent bath and sleeping loft that is reached by a ship's ladder and is lit by the hipped dormer windows. The eccentric windows of the two guest rooms step up in counterpoint to the curved trellis below and orchestrate the "andante" rhythms requested by the owners, music lovers who sometimes used that language to conjure up more expressive images.

In the New England coastal tradition, weathered white cedar shingles encase the lighthouse from top to bottom and flow across its inflected curves. The trim and trellis are cedar stained white. Inside, with the exception of oak flooring and a fir kitchen, all is painted a nautical white to complete the imagery of a stately island residence, with a welcome touch of whimsy.

This house was published in the "country homes" issue of *Architectural Digest* two years after it was completed. Among the calls and letters I received from readers, one stood out from all the rest. It was a handwritten note from a prisoner in a state institution who, after apologizing for his forwardness in communicating with me, proceeded to tell me that this was the house he dreamed of at night alone in his cell. I occasionally remember his words when I reflect on the house, and am moved again by them.

JUSTUS HOUSE

Hinsdale, Illinois
1992–93

In the early spring of 1992 a couple, contemporaries of mine, asked me to come to their bilevel house in the Chicago suburbs to discuss designing a new house for them on a site a few blocks away. On a blustery March day we sat down around their kitchen table to discuss the usual contractual procedures for designing and then producing contract documents for a new house. As we reviewed what that entailed in time and therefore fees, Dan told me that he was interviewing local builders. He expected that they, rather than general contractors, would have the expertise to construct the house using in-house personnel for services such as structural and mechanical work, thereby reducing fees. He and his wife, Barbara, had added to their present house with hands-on attention, and they were prepared to do the same now in order to pour all their available funds into the project itself.

Both of their professions allowed them the flexibility to supervise the construction, and Dan promised that if I agreed to produce just the design documents, he would ensure that they were faithfully followed. He would call and we would consult by phone, facsimile, or in person whenever any design issues arose during the construction process. I had agreed to similar conditions for the design of Wit's End except that my firm had assisted in selecting the contractor and had done all the field supervision, including working with the mechanical subcontractor to engineer a system that not only functioned well but was well integrated into the design aesthetic of the house. I was very reluctant to undertake an even more minimal involvement with strangers; however, Chicago was still deep in the recession, I liked them, and their program was an intriguing one. I began work on a handshake.

After much searching in the neighborhood the couple had found a deep

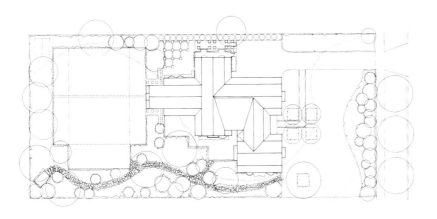

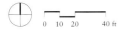
0 10 20   40 ft

lot on a wide tree-lined street that faced the typical mix of pre–World War II houses found anywhere within a thirty-mile radius of the city. All of them, whether faced in wood, masonry, or stucco, were of a common scale that was appropriate to the size of their lot, and all shared a common setback. Each as well had a unique physiognomy that revealed their European antecedents, whether English Georgian, French Normandy, or Dutch Colonial. This was a street that had yet to fall prey to the tear-down syndrome that affected many sought-after suburbs. My clients were to be one of the first on the street to take advantage of the newest zoning by tearing down a 1950s two-story brick-and-board ranch house that had undoubtedly replaced an earlier and smaller dwelling.

This particular suburb, Hinsdale, which straddled the Cook County line twenty miles west of Chicago, was settled over a century and a half ago by pioneers who followed the old Black Hawk Indian trail toward the setting sun, seeking the high ground west of Lake Michigan. During the Civil War an entrepreneur bought six-thousand-plus acres of land and plotted a village grid of north-south streets that he named for the presidents and east-west ones that were numbered. All the parkways were planted with shade trees, and in the center of town close to the railhead early residents built a vintage collection of clapboard Victorians. The land around the village was farmed until the westward expansion of the Chicago suburbs filled in the surrounding acreage, and a number of the very earliest homes in the village were built in the vernacular of these Illinois farmhouses. Lapped siding covered the two-story frame houses whose muntinized windows were symmetrically set below gabled roofs. The Victorian influence caused an exuberant breakout of the box as the Queen Anne style of the late nine-

0   5   10   20 ft

feet wide, and village zoning laws decreed that one-quarter of that dimension be devoted to side-yard setbacks. This meant that the planning for the garage and drive would be tight.

But before I could begin to solve the puzzle of the front facade, I had to resolve a program with my clients that listed a plethora of different rooms accompanied by a budget that would allow for the construction of only about three-quarters of them. With two adult children and a third in secondary school, Barbara was anticipating a house that in the future would be filled with grandchildren, and so the couple was up- rather than downsizing. It also made sense for resalability to build a house of a size commensurate with the hipped-roof "McMansions" that were cropping up around the neighborhood, especially one that contained the classic want list of the 1990s. The couple had also prepared a relational bubble diagram that disposed the majority of the first-floor rooms around the kitchen. That room also required natural light and access to a terrace and herb garden. Fortunately, because of a further village zoning code that restricted the size of the house's footprint, they had decided that the master bedroom would occupy the second floor. However, the first-floor plan needed to be flexible enough to provide for the possibility of converting a room on that floor to that purpose should a future need arise. We decided that the family room would be the designated swing space.

As I scanned the list of rooms looking for ways to consolidate them, I thought of how often in other country houses I had designed I had commingled the living and dining rooms so that each shared a sense of a larger volume. Since the program called for both an additional family room and an eat-in, lounge-in kitchen, it seemed logical that the two lesser-used rooms be combined.

teenth century added turrets, wraparound porches, and other asymmetrical appendages. After World War I, houses took on a more sober aspect and returned to generally symmetrical facades aligned along the street. My clients' property, located eight blocks south of the center on Washington Street, belonged to such a neighborhood.

Dan and Barbara wanted their new house to respect neighborhood tradition by maintaining a similar presence on the street, with the exception that a two-car attached garage would be added. However, the other three sides had no such constraints. I would be free to pursue more unique forms on the sides and rear as I strove to maximize the number of rooms that would take advantage of the southern exposure. One other stipulation made by my clients was that the garage doors be invisible from the street and that I try to use as much of the existing driveway as possible, while saving a perennial flowerbed planted along its northern edge. Most of the older houses on the block had their detached garages placed at the rear, so that the entirety of their front facades looked over the street. My clients' lot was only one hundred

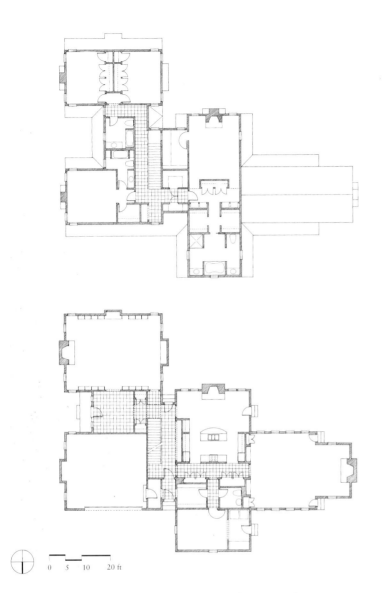

What seemed even more reasonable was that the library should integrate itself into these rooms as well, so that the dining table could serve as a reference table and the lounge seating of the living room could serve for reading as well as conversation. Since the ubiquitous television was to be confined to the family room, this consolidation of three separate rooms into one multipurpose room was agreeable to the couple. The important dimension was one that would allow the dining-room table to expand during the holidays to its maximum length of fourteen feet. When serving space was added to each end of the table, the overall dimension became

the same as that needed to comfortably park a car. Since both spaces functionally required the same width, the symmetrical two-story street front was solved in plan by pairing the multipurpose room with the attached garage on the opposite side of the entry foyer. Barbara's desire for a room of her own was satisfied by allotting it a pivotal spot, not unlike one assigned to the estate manager in another day. It was attached to the side of the house so that it overlooked the tradesman's entrance as well as the driveway, also accessing the rear gardens.

In reality, the plan that evolved did indeed become an ordered three-

dimensional version of their graphic diagram as consolidated. The plan was made intentionally axial as well as cross-axial in its disposition of rooms, in order to establish vistas onto the landscape while ordering procession through the rooms perspectivally, a device to further reinforce the plan's relationship to traditional antecedents.

The other, blocky houses fronting on their street lack the first-floor family room and large eat-in kitchen required by this fin-de-siècle generation. The addition of those rooms to the ground floor unbalances the square footage of the first versus second floor, thereby precluding the development of a house as a simple box. What lends itself to the natural resolution of that proportional problem is the archetypal stepped basilica form, reminiscent of the farm buildings once present in the surrounding countryside. What also appealed to me about that shape was Barbara's Dutch ancestry and strong affinity for the forms of the Low Countries. The gabled ends of the two "basilicas" aligned along the street reminded me of the town houses that line the canals of Amsterdam. If the facades followed a more curvilinear transition at the setback from the first to second floor, and if the roof dropped below them, the similarity would be even more striking. Once that relationship was presented to the couple, they painted the front door Delft blue to further the association.

Even though my clients were prepared for the other three facades to deviate from their traditional dictum for the front, I realized that variations on the basilica forms created for that front facade could in fact be repeated on the side and rear facades as well. Thus the house reinterprets a historical form, not only evoking memories but, by the fourfold reiteration of that historical form, presenting an appearance unique in its own time.

THE PRESERVE

New Buffalo, Michigan
1987–93

Late in the winter of 1987, as Wit's End was nearing completion in Sawyer, Michigan, I was contacted by Madeline Reinke, the innkeeper of the Inn at Union Pier, a bed-and-breakfast located in a neighboring town. We often convened contractor meetings for Wit's End in the inn's sunroom, and Madeline and her husband, Bill, had been watching the building process unfold. The couple wanted me to remodel an adjacent property that they planned to annex to the inn.

Born in New Buffalo, Madeline was the third generation raised in Harbor Country and the first in

recent memory to open a luxury inn to cater to Chicagoans beginning to rediscover this tranquil region in southern Michigan. The area was very popular in the early part of the century, when the train from Chicago made numerous stops along the lake's southwestern shore. The original inn was a stalwart clapboard box built in the 1910s, its two stories stained a dark eggshell blue and trimmed in white enamel. Inside, the high-ceilinged lounge had a comfortable collection of slipcovered chairs grouped in clusters around the field-stone fireplace. While its ambience was still that of the bygone era of natural fir ceilings darkened with age

and stained oak floors, its rooms had been remodeled to include ceramic Swedish stoves (kakelughs), soft down comforters, and whirlpool tubs. It was the 1980s, and classic Sears Roebuck frame bungalows along Lake Shore Road were being purchased for back taxes by local entrepreneurs, who winterized and then resold them to those Chicagoans who were anxiously searching for the peaceful retreats still available in small-town America. Owners of old resort inns on Lake Michigan with rows of small detached cottages were selling them off as condominium units to young Chicagoans eager to

the rooms, brought the building up to code, and added a two-story lattice-framed porch to its east side, along with a boardwalk to link it to the original building. Bill acted as the general contractor, and the transformation was completed in mid-June, in time for an open house the couple organized to celebrate the inn's second anniversary.

During the remodeling process, Madeline spoke often of a 175-acre parcel of wetlands that her grandfather had purchased in the early 1900s, seventy-five years after the Indian Treaty of 1833 made Berrien County available for settlement. Madeline's

duck blinds who drove their four-wheel-drive pickups in along an old dirt road at the base of the embankment had ever disturbed its solitude.

Madeline and her two brothers, Jim and Ralph Sima, shared the Sima family dream of developing the fifty acres of high ground in the center of the site. The family was very conscious of the ecological importance of the property, since it was not only a known habitat for the blue heron but had been designated by the Department of Natural Resources as the third largest wetlands in the state of Michigan. Located on both the Great Lakes and Mississippi flyways, the Galien River Basin was visited by thousands of birds during the spring and fall migrations.

watch the sun go down over the lake on summer evenings from their screened porches.

My new clients were fortunate that the street on which the inn sat had other larger houses along its tree-lined avenue, since it was their neighbor to the west that they had acquired. This house had been a part of the original inn complex built by the first owner in the 1910s and 1920s. The hipped-roof foursquare clapboard looked like it too came from the pages of the Sears catalog since it resembled other similar types extant in the older Chicago suburbs. It reconfigured easily into the inn's annex as we quickly reproportioned

property was located at the mouth of the Galien River in New Buffalo, the adjoining town to the south. The river wound through the site, flowing into the lake through the newly dredged harbor. Clapboard condominiums called South Cove (designed by Harry Weese) were rising to ring the half-moon harbor. The tracks of a railroad freight line that passed through the town also ran alongside a portion of the marshy land. The high embankment formed for the roadbed effectively shut off the site from the Red Arrow Highway to the east, the old roadway that parallels the lake, linking all these Harbor Country towns. Only hunters tending their

The high ground had already been checked by archaeologists for possible traces of the Pokagon Potawatomi Indians, who had apparently set up summer encampments on the land. Several sites on the bluff had yielded artifacts that had been identified and radio-carbon-dated to the fifteenth to seventeenth centuries. This was important because this particular branch of the Potawatomi had never been given formal recognition by the United States government. Their descendants needed to prove they had inhabited the region to achieve national status as an Indian tribe in order to take advantage of the protections given by federal law and normalizing relations with the Bureau of Indian Affairs. The Simas hoped their land would provide enough evidence for the Pokagon to achieve this status.

One cold and cloudy Saturday afternoon, Madeline and I decided to explore the property. We trekked in along the old dirt track until it petered out short of the site and then plowed through tangled undergrowth until we reached the base of the wooded plateau and climbed to the top. Through the trees we looked out over acres of dried cattails and yellowed marsh grasses. In the distance the

cal covenants they then incorporated into the master deed.

I had been entrusted with the design of the stone pillars and gate at the entry, as well as with the River Villas, which they planned to build in stages with proceeds from the sale of the building sites. At the dedication I presented renderings of the clapboard units, which were variations of the Michigan vernacular of the region. However, although the road into the Preserve began a few blocks from the harbor in town, it also ran for a full mile along the uninhabited wetlands before it reached the building sites. Apparently their isolation, coupled with price tags that reflected their exclusivity, discouraged most potential buyers. The concept of the River Villas was eventually abandoned, the building type being considered incompatible with the type of clientele expected to be attracted to the homesites. The land set aside for them was then converted into additional building sites. But still the lots sat unpurchased, except for one wooded one that faced due west across the Galien River Basin to Lake Michigan. This site was sold to a couple who commuted between Chicago and Hong Kong and clearly valued the solitude of the Preserve.

As construction began on this lot, the Galien River Associates (as the Sima family had incorporated itself) decided that certain amenities needed to be added to the complex to attract additional buyers and to appease the one in residence. I was then commissioned in early 1993 to design a clubhouse to accompany the pool and tennis court that were planned for the center of the site. Since revenue was scarce, I was asked to devise an economical design that would accommodate changing rooms for the pool and a large screened room with a stone fireplace for Preserve residents and friends. I centered the building between the court and the pool and designed a structure with a

river, a leaden gray line that reflected the sky, flowed slowly through them. I shivered in the sharp icy wind that blew off the lake across the hilltop as Madeline, seemingly impervious to the penetrating cold, paced off a portion of the site for the future family homestead. On the way back out of the swampy tract we lost the trail in the gathering darkness and wandered endlessly in that desolate marsh until eventually we bumped into the railroad embankment and numbly followed it out and into town.

I was reminded of that frozen adventure on a spring day four years later when Madeline, with her first-born son, Willy, aged two, invited me to see their stewardship of the newly developed property. A gravel road ran for a mile on a narrow strip of land between the embankment and the wetlands and then climbed to encircle the tableland, where twenty housing sites had been identified and tagged with green-and-white birdhouses that were mounted on poles with the site num-

ber painted on their sides. The family also planned to erect a series of semi-attached multifamily residences they had dubbed the "River Villas" at the base of the upland facing out over a fork in the river. The units would add an additional twenty families—a number of inhabitants far below that allowed by local zoning codes, but one that they hoped would be small enough to be absorbed into the ecosystem of the wetlands. After the tour, I sat with Madeline, Bill, Jimmy, and Ralph in a small frame house just outside the entry to the property, which they had purchased as a future sales office. We tossed about possible names for the site and eventually chose "The Preserve." In fact, a year later in May, when the road was paved and the press packets assembled, they formally announced their pledge that in perpetuity 120 acres of the land would be designated as a preserve and named, after their father, the Louis J. Sima Nature Preserve and Wildlife Habitat. These environmental and archaeologi-

simple gabled roof supported by exposed prefab wood trusses that would also cover outdoor decks to shelter spectators from the summer sun. Men's and women's bathrooms accessible from within or without flanked the central room and storage areas; sliding barn doors completed either end. Inside, the roof trusses, side braces, and window trim were painted gray while the beaded-board wall panels typical of the Michigan resort palette were painted in white enamel. The exterior clapboard siding, cedar shingled roof, and riverbed stone chimneys completed the vernacular character of the clubhouse's 2,500 square feet. Finally, a secondary small pool-equipment building designed in the same vernacular was placed on the cross-axis across the pool and centered on the club house. This building drew the eye across the pool, extending the main building's vistas into the landscape. The Preserve was thus prepared to welcome new members.

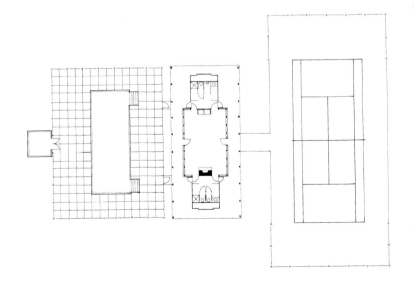

0 10 20   40 ft

REINKE RESIDENCE

New Buffalo, Michigan
1993–95

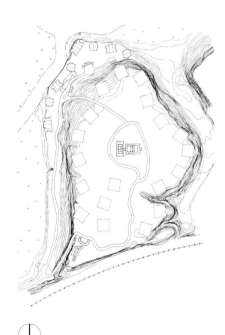

Shortly before the clubhouse at the Preserve was started, Madeline Reinke had a second child, Louise, named for her grandfather. Just as the new baby began to stretch the capacity of the family's current house next door to the Inn at Union Pier, some friends came up with an offer to purchase the house. Since Madeline had also announced that the next generation would not end with Louise, it became increasingly apparent that their five-year expansion plan needed to be accelerated. This meant selecting her site in the Preserve and building the house she had envisioned with me on that memorable afternoon six years before. Galien River Associates had also decided that additional residences on the site would dissipate the sense of isolation they feared was deterring buyers. Madeline and her married brother, Jimmy, agreed to build on the land, and each selected a site for their family com-

pound. Typically, Madeline and Bill chose what they felt might be the least saleable one. Although it was on the upland and faced the wetlands, the approach road climbed up to it, curving about on two sides, and the railroad tracks, although sunken, formed its third border. Madeline added up all the positive attributes of the triangular site: since it was the first property staked out on the plateau, it would be the command post looking out over all who passed by. Her children would also learn to love the sound of the train whistling up for the New Buffalo crossing a mile away, and the sight of it accelerating past their property along the tracks below the crest of their hill.

As her children required more of her time, Madeline realized that it was time to relinquish her duties as innkeeper. Bill, too, had been occupied in forging new sales territories for his company, so when a Chicago

couple offered to buy the inn after spending a couple of weekends there, the couple reluctantly agreed to sell. Madeline's and Bill's relatives then became the recipients of her hospitality, and the housing and entertainment of the extended family a priority in the program for the new house. This family included, in addition to their own children, Bill's sister, who lived with them, as well as his older daughter from a previous marriage. These two, it was decided, would share an apartment over the garage, linked to the main house but also accessed by exterior stairs. The garage itself was planned to hold two cars and a boat, which the family would use to take prospective buyers upriver from the harbor to the home sites.

The family association had developed building envelopes of one hundred by one hundred feet for each site, and the couple was determined to abide by their square footage

allotment. Since the significant view was the one that faced south over the wetlands, we needed to consider a plan that would fit inside the envelope while simultaneously emphasizing that exposure. This entailed siting the house parallel to the entry road, which forked just before it began its climb up to the plateau. The left fork ran along the riverbank to the site of the proposed River Villas. The right fork followed along the edge of their lot and curved around it as it reached the top. We located the short driveway at that point and, to avoid taking up more of the land, planned that the three individual garage doors would face the road, not unlike a carriage house with quarters above. All the public rooms were to be stretched out along the ridge to face the marsh, which left the private rooms to face the rear yard, where children could be monitored at play.

Some clients collect pictures of

objects, rooms, or entire houses that interest them. Madeline and Bill had no such clippings, nor had they any preconceptions. The house's appearance, they stated, was secondary to the larger issues of the interrelationships within the family and, in turn, the relationship with their land. Since we had successfully worked together on a number of projects, I too was not concerned about its appearance at first but concentrated on putting together a workable plan. As I analyzed the program, it seemed plausible to consider the public and private zones as two unique rectangular blocks that became tangential at a certain point. The couple did not want the house to appear too grand, and this resolution of the two slipped rectangles permitted each one to have its own smaller hipped roof. The two roofs were separated by valleys drained by crickets at the point of tangency. These staggered rectangles also reduced the apparent size of the front facade by setting the entry block back from the garage block, thereby forming a forecourt.

In developing the initial square footage and plans, I had to keep in mind Madeline's penchant for exuberant forms, which had manifested itself in the past in the purchase of two extraordinarily large overstuffed sofas and accompanying lounge chairs, whose sizes dictated a very commodious living room. This important room would be the focus of family events. It was to be a light-filled place where parents could socialize but simultaneously watch their children, and it was to be a place from which everyone could watch the seasons change over the Preserve. It needed to be at the southwest end of the public rectangle to maximize its exposure, but this meant that the dining room, another public room, would fall between it and the front entrance. This rather unconventional format suited the

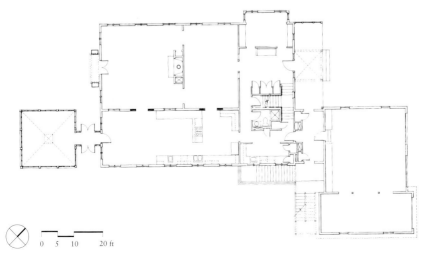

0 5 10   20 ft

couple, who decided that the dining room would be the recipient of the signature Swedish stove used at their inn. This would add to its stature, but at the same time meant reinforcing the floor to accept its two-and-one-half-ton load.

The juxtaposition of the two rectangles also meant that the family kitchen in the private block could extend along the entire length of the two public rooms and would face east to capture the morning sun. This condition worked conventionally by connecting dining room and kitchen, and less conventionally by connecting the living and family rooms, which resolved the adult requirement to supervise children at play during parties. Madeline then headquartered her desk in the private family zone, while Bill chose the public sector for his study, preferring to settle just off the entry foyer where he was easily accessible to visitors. Madeline's next concern was to sufficiently size and position the private "back of the yard" spaces, the laundry and mudroom and so forth. I had connected these areas to the garage by a covered breezeway, so that callers could either step onto the front porch to knock on the front door or walk through to the rear door. Each entry accessed the same stairway. Upstairs, public and private space merged in the two blocks as Madeline and Bill established their master suite above the living room and added three children's bedrooms in anticipation of the arrival of Raymond.

Mindful of the budget, I had worked out a room module that was

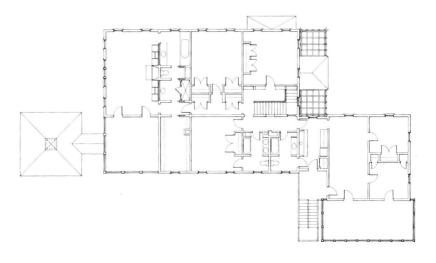

western score. Bill enclosed a screened sleeping porch off the master bedroom to avoid the potential pitfalls of an exposed deck sitting over a heated room below—which occurred when the family room was extended an additional sixteen feet to accommodate both indoor dining and a children's play area. Each expansion, though initially met with mock exasperation, was always correct when it came to creating a workable plan for the extended family.

Having acted as the general contractor on all the remodelings of the inn, Bill wasn't anxious to repeat those duties for his own house. But as the program expanded, he realized that only in reassuming that role would he save the money necessary to build the house they would find satisfactory. He also decided to be the field superintendent, thereby reducing our time on the job and his expenses even further.

Although I too, like Madeline and Bill, had no preconceived notions about any stylistic predilection for the house, I knew that it would express Madeline's Michigan roots and Bill's adopted ones. It would be commodious, but also practical, sensible, and basically as simple as the large frame buildings I remembered from two childhood summers. These sites of reverie had been located at a lakeside church camp in the rolling dunes of Bridgman, fifteen miles to the north. Indeed, the long side facade reminds me in subtle ways of the girls' dormitory at that camp, although at the time I designed it this was not a conscious memory. The house's most obvious ancestor was the old Inn at Union Pier. The blocky form of the inn (although clad in clapboard rather than in shingles) made it another one of the "tight little boxes under the wind" that Vincent Scully referred to in writing about the Middle Western context of our own cottage, Boardwalk. Because of the couple's desire for modesty, we decided to stain the house to blend in with the bark of the

easy to construct and had also organized the upstairs plumbing in close proximity to that of the downstairs. One of our few extravagances had been to increase the height of the first-floor ceilings to ten feet to allow for the extra light that transomed windows and doors would add, a height that was also an appropriate proportion for the large rooms. It was difficult to keep the square footage from mounting. The breezeway was annexed to the mudroom. Bill's study projected out a bay on the side facade. A cupola appeared on the garage roof while eyebrow windows on the main roofs introduced a classical note into the otherwise Mid-

surrounding trees on the wooded site. The warm, dark gray was also a practical color that complemented the fieldstone base as it would the soon-to-be-weathered cedar shingle roof. This color scheme, coupled with the choice of shingles for roof as well as siding, gave the house a sense of completeness, in that all of its parts were subsumed into the whole.

A year or so after the family moved into the house, Madeline was quoted in an article about the house: "We're always discovering nuances of Margaret's design. She has so much knowledge as to what makes a home livable, like the way the spaces flow into each other. Each season,

this home just gets better and better. It's a great place for a growing family, and it inspires me."

How typical of Madeline to be so generous in her praise when, in fact, it is people like her who inspire me and make me sorry when our association ends, as it did the summer day we photographed her house for *Traditional Home* magazine. That afternoon Madeline told me that Bill had been promoted and transferred to another state. Such a possibility had never occurred to me. I assumed that she would be the chatelaine of the Preserve forever, but the house traded hands the following summer.

NINETEENTH-CENTURY FARMHOUSE

*Rockford, Illinois
1992–94*

It was in the late summer of 1992 that a prospective client, Yvonne, called to ask diffidently if I could possibly drive out to Rockford the next day to inspect a nineteenth-century house that was for sale. She explained that she and her husband were moving to this city on the Rock River, ninety miles northwest of Chicago, from Lancaster, Pennsylvania. After an exhaustive and unsatisfactory search through builder subdivisions in the suburb of Loves Park where they planned to settle, this old house on five acres of land was the only property that she had found suitable. Wedged between two subdivisions, it and several other homesteads of equal size were the only large sites left in the suburb. Over the years, she explained, the house had suffered from the addition of several poorly conceived as well as poorly executed constructions. Could I come and consult with her as to whether I felt it was salvageable?

I am always intrigued by good old buildings, especially mistreated ones. I like to rescue them. As I reveal or reinforce the intention of the original master builder, I create a bridge that spans the years between us. Such a building may have been conceived by another architect whose work I admire; I was at that time restoring a suburban country club designed in 1928 by the firm that had descended from Daniel Burnham. Or it may have been constructed by a local carpenter or craftsperson from plans sold in pattern books or plans of their own creation that interpreted the style most in fashion at the time. All are candidates for my care. In this instance Yvonne's discovery fell into the latter category. I drove out to Rockford that next afternoon to see standing on a grassy hillock a small but striking stone house designed in the Greek Revival style. Attached to it on three sides were unsympathetic additions, but the house's essential

dignity shone through them. It had the strong presence often found in representatives of that formal style. This one had an oddly proportioned facade, almost folklike. The windows on the front were not symmetrically disposed about the center gable, as would be typical of that tradition, and the muntinized double-hung originals had been replaced by panes of inoperable clear glass. But underneath the current coat of gray paint were the same solid sandstone blocks that were visible on the interior. Quarried a foot and a half thick, they were the basic load-bearing building blocks of the house, their size yielding deep window recesses that brought soft light into the rooms.

In contrast, the twentieth-century wood-frame additions, of which there were at least three, were flimsy. Every material used, or construction method employed, was cheap and expedient, from the two-by-four studs to the scored plywood siding. There was

nothing original left on the interior of the stone house either. Even the old staircase was missing, having been replaced by a rustic prefab one that spiraled down from the second floor to the unfinished basement.

The house was sited above the confluence of two small streams that flowed across the rear of the property. In order to optimize views of these rivulets, new projections had been built that angled off the back, thereby blocking the sun from reaching the interior rooms. There were two living rooms, one in the old section that was bereft of its original hearth, and another in the new section with a prefab fireplace. Only one bedroom existed, a loftlike space at the top of the circular stair in the old stone structure in which someone had built a walk-in closet across the back wall, blocking off any views from the rear windows. The kitchen, although large, was internalized, its decor dark, its appliances arranged in an awkward manner. Since it was also the first room seen from the front entrance, it was a shame that a succession of owners had had so little understanding of architectural history or such minimal access to architects that they would have added on to the old house in such an appalling fashion. My hands itched with the desire to tear off all the new additions that suffocatingly surrounded the original house and build anew.

I voiced the urge to Yvonne as we closed the door on the real-estate agent and walked to our cars, but she explained that her funds were limited and undoubtedly didn't cover such a dire act. "Should I buy it? Can the place really be renovated while still keeping the additions?" she asked. I looked back across the acres of lush landscape. Beyond the silhouette of a crumbling concrete silo, whose cylindrical form was all that remained of the old barn, sat the old house, silently contained within its contemporary shackles. A pair of golden retrievers stood like sentinels beside the front door, their tails slowly wagging as they watched us walk away. "You can't make a silk purse out of that sow's ear," I commented "without seriously opening your purse strings." I regretfully advised her not to buy it.

I had liked Yvonne immediately upon meeting her. At one point during our tour of the old house she had admitted to me, quite matter of factly but with a quiet smile, that I had appeared in answer to a prayer. I didn't know quite how to respond to that admission, but it was a humbling thought. As I drove the ninety miles back to Chicago, I briefly regretted advising her to abandon the old house. I wanted to save it as much for my own sake as for hers. I spent the rest of the long journey figuring out just how I would restore it if it were mine. When she called a few days later to tell me that she and her husband, Jim, had decided to buy it anyway and to ask me if I would still

consider fixing it up in spite of my reservations, I felt a deep satisfaction that its fate was being placed in my hands after all. By that time, if I could convince her to do it, I already knew just how to rehabilitate it.

The sellers had left behind an old photograph of the stone house and a notebook containing information on its history that had been passed along from owner to owner. It appeared to have been commissioned in the 1850s by the wife of a man who sent her the proceeds from a mining claim he had staked out during the California gold rush of 1849. He included with his bank draft a letter instructing her to "build us a house on a spot where two creeks come together." She did and selected the prevailing Greek Revival style for her new one-thousand-square-foot house. A local craftsman undoubtedly interpreted the style for her and, while lacking the perfect symmetries and proportions a classically trained architect would have brought to it, crafted it with care and imbued it with that powerful naive presence I had felt when I first encountered it. Apparently the house had remained virtually unchanged for over a century and, even though abandoned for some years during the Great Depression, maintained enough of its original character to be listed by the Illinois Historic Landmarks Survey in 1974. Later in the decade the first of two revisions occurred: the addition of the new entry/kitchen wing off the west side and the sun porch that covered the front, cutting off south light from the living room. A few years later, the addition of the second living room above a garage doubled the size of the west wing while completing the building's fall from grace. To resurrect it became my personal crusade.

I began to study our "as built" plans to determine how I could convert the interior of the existing complex into the more conventional three-bedroom house Yvonne had requested. This configuration would ensure its resale value, since the couple had a history of remaining in one spot for no longer than a few years. Jim's job as a company comptroller had taken them as far afield as the Far East, where they had amassed a handsome collection of Japanese Tonsu chests. While I was sketching, Yvonne began searching for a contractor whose work would pass her exacting standards. A local builder looked over some of our initial schemes and concurred with our opinion that it would cost as much to drastically remodel the additions as it would to tear the first floor down to the decking and rebuild a sturdier

version on virtually the same footprint. He would save the lower level, which included a three-car garage, mechanical rooms, and some assorted odd spaces that could be used as a sauna, wine cellar, and office. This level, because the land sloped down to the streams, was accessible from a lower deck. The existing windows could be adapted somewhat to the symmetrical spacing desired in the new addition above. The builder, Ron, prepared a preliminary budget that, although it stretched their budget, was essentially acceptable to my clients. I prepared drawings that illustrated my initial plan.

My hope from the beginning had been to design a new structure that would balance harmoniously with the old and in the process restore the old to its original dignified state. What I had identified as the essential architectural problem when I first looked

at the house was the need to restructure the additions in such a way that the new two-thirds did not overshadow the original third, as it had previously. This was accomplished by constructing a flat roof over the new center third, still the entry/kitchen section, so that it acted as a traditional "hyphen" separating the new end third, which would become the bedroom wing with a gable roof corresponding to that of the old house. The columned entry, pilasters, and pedimented gable on this clapboard addition used the classical vocabulary of the original Greek Revival style, which also included muntinized windows and large-scale cornices. The old front door was eliminated from the original house and replaced by a window that centered itself underneath the one above, as the door had not. A new fireplace was added to this front, following the asymmetrical pairs of windows up beyond the second floor, where the chimney jogged back on one side to meet the gable in the center. The new westernmost third was brought forward five feet to align with the old. This served a dual purpose. It increased the interior space, thereby permitting the inclusion of two large bedrooms in that wing, and it allowed the entry to appear recessed back from the two paired gables, thus balancing the composition and establishing the old house's parity with the new. Since the budget permitted neither the use of stone on the new addition nor sandblasting the limestone on the original, the entire complex was unified by painting it a "sandstone" color. Yvonne herself supervised the interior finishing. An artist as well as an amateur photographer, she faux-painted a "stone" floor at the base of the basement stairs where the cats hung out and chose a soft sand color for the walls that echoed the exterior stone. A sense of quiet, order, and strength seemed to prevail inside and out, reconnecting the reconstructed house with the spirit of its classical ancestors.

Yvonne and Jim had spent their first full year in the house at the close of the summer of 1995 when the word came that *Architectural Digest* had accepted the remodeling for their February "before and after" issue. Professional photographs needed to be taken immediately. Although Yvonne, the perfectionist, said she had yet to find the appropriate landscape architect to interpret her vision of the land, she agreed to scatter some rye grass seed in the bare spots left by the construction process so that we could proceed with the photography before the leaves turned. We enjoyed renewing our acquaintance during the photography session those last days of summer, but she sadly confided to me that Jim's job demands might necessitate a relocation. A short time after the article was published, I received a call from a real-estate agent asking certain questions about the construction of the house. A prospective buyer also called to question me about my fees for enlarging the house yet again—she appeared amazed that Yvonne's program had left out the ubiquitous family room. I almost reminded her that one hundred years ago a whole family had been raised in the original one thousand square feet of the small stone house.

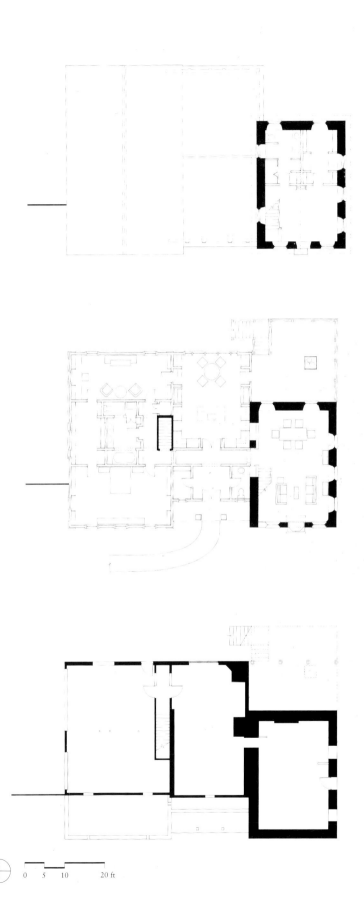

0   5   10   20 ft

PRAIRIE CROSSING

Grayslake, Illinois
1992–99

As I work on Prairie Crossing, I find that I am learning a lot about how the home-building industry in Chicago analyzes what American families want in a new house. This ecologically sensitive conservation community is being developed in Grayslake, Illinois, a village of nine square miles located within Libertyville township some forty miles northwest of Chicago. Hired jointly by Shaw Homes, the builder, and by Prairie Holdings Corporation, the owner of the 667-acre parcel of Illinois farm and prairie land, I am one of a team of three architects that has designed a series of middle-income, single-family houses for the development. Our designs, done individually, are intended to stylistically support the vernacular of this portion of Lake County, a former farming region now considered a suburb of Chicago.

In spite of the fact that Prairie Crossing was named in part for the intersecting rail lines of the Milwaukee and the Wisconsin Central Rail-

roads that cross on its western border, the village of Grayslake became a commuter suburb only over the course of the last twenty years, as large corporations left Chicago to form a new commercial corridor stretching north from Chicago's O'Hare Airport along the Tri-state Tollway. While traditional suburban towns along the North Shore of Lake Michigan (such as the one I grew up in) experienced normal growth in the 1980s and 1990s, Grayslake, further inland, tripled in size in the same time span. It would have tripled yet again if concerned citizens who owned large tracts of open lands in the area, some for generations, had not banded together to control the population density of their community and preserve its endangered wetlands and virgin prairies. The topology of the land was fixed after the last glacial era, twelve thousand years ago, that formed the many lakes that gave the county its name. Native grasses dating back to that

time that grew only beside glacial springs have been found in a neighboring prairie.

Prairie Holdings Corporation, a consortium of eight families, was formed in 1987 to buy the controversial site, once part of a 2,200-acre parcel owned by a Chicago developer since the early 1970s. Naming it Heartland, he had submitted plans to the Lake County board for a development that would have added fifteen thousand people to a village one-third that size. (On the subsequent Prairie Crossing site alone, he planned to build 1,600 houses.) His schemes were rejected by the board, and a lawsuit ensued whereby the county and local governments made an effort to curtail his high-density plans in order to moderate population growth and prevent the destruction of the ecology of the site. The litigation lasted fifteen years, finally reaching the U.S. Supreme Court, which agreed to limitations on the number of houses that could be built

on the parcel. The developer subsequently sold the Prairie Crossing site to the Prairie Holdings Corporation, which was led by local conservationists Gaylord and Dorothy Donnelley, who had opposed him.

Prairie Holdings Corporation, with Gaylord's nephew, George A. Ranney Jr., a lawyer, as president, then hired landscape architecture firms, land planners, engineers, resource managers, and wetlands consultants to lay out only 317 homesites of varying sizes in varying clusters, either around a small, 22-acre lake in the center of the property or near adjoining marshes or prairies. They planned for ten miles of hiking and riding trails throughout the parcel as well as the preservation of a 150-acre working farm that would yield fresh, organically grown vegetables for members of the community. They intended not only to conserve the land but to use ecologically sound energy and materials in the houses. Prairie and wetlands restorations

would filter storm-water drainage from the site into the lake, thereby saving the nearby village the expense of storm sewers. Farming windbreaks consisting of rows of maple trees crossing the site on east-west and north-south axes would also be preserved and enhanced. Prairie Crossing would become the first community in the nation to adopt Building America, a unique partnership between the residential home-building industry and the Department of Energy designed to develop new technologies for energy conservation, ensuring 50 percent less energy consumption than comparably sized houses in other subdivisions.

By 1992, when the architects were hired, the infrastructure was in place for Prairie Crossing. As development manager, the corporation had chosen the Shaw Company, whose president, Charles Shaw, was also slated for the presidency of the Urban Land Institute. Shaw Homes, an affiliate of the company, would be the builder. Its president, Frank Martin, and Victoria Post Ranney, a vice-president of Prairie Holdings and wife of George Ranney (and a landscape historian who had worked on the Frederick Law Olmsted papers), interviewed a number of architects before selecting the final triad.

For my interview, I took Vicky and Frank to Harbor Country in the fall of 1992 to see Boardwalk and Wit's End. Frank was surprised at the amount of living space I had packed into the small houses. Wit's End is especially deceiving in scale, appearing to be twice its 2,300-square-foot size. The only criticism of that house he voiced, from a builder's standpoint, was the lack of a breakfast room in the kitchen and the paucity of closet space—two elements their marketing-research studies deemed essential.

The other two architects selected, James Nagle and Frederick Phillips, happened to be friends of mine, and together we would eventually develop over eighteen housing types representing, in varying degrees, the vernacular of the nineteenth-century Illinois farmhouse on the exterior while providing, within varying price ranges, all the late-twentieth-century amenities desired by the typical purchaser in the interior. Working as a team, we accepted certain parameters, such as eight-in-twelve gabled-roof pitches, clapboard siding, and double-hung windows, and we also agreed to develop a common set of detail sheets to include wall sections, roof overhangs, chimney types, and so forth.

In the initial stages, our designs related to four distinctly different types of lots. The smallest plots are laid out in the "Village," which has a street grid surrounding a green that overlooks the lake. The next larger lots, the "Prairie" homesites, are arranged in the midst of prairie land in pinwheel clusters of eight. Still larger, "Meadow" sites are strung out in curving loops facing prairies and

wetlands, and the largest sites, the "Field" lots, form lines along the perimeter of the development and face the farmland that surrounds the entire site. All the house lots together comprise less than 40 percent of the land.

Rick Phillips developed schemes for the largest Field lots, whose sizes allowed a certain latitude with respect to the placement of garages and other appendages. Cognizant of marketing studies, his first designs closely interpreted the generic Georgians that were considered the most popular and saleable suburban housing type. However, they soon sported front-porch options, connecting them more closely to the country character of the complex. Jim Nagle chose to produce a collection of vernacular Midwestern cottages for the Village lots, his preferred type. Although the smallest in size, these lots were the only ones laid out with old-fashioned alleys that allowed for attached garages at the rear, thus preserving the front facade in its entirety. This was an especially important aspect, since "curb appeal" is a classic marketing strategy.

I tackled the medium-sized lots. Their basic proportions, 70 feet wide by approximately 125 feet deep, meant that, with setbacks, a house and a two-car attached garage placed side by side needed to coexist in a 55-foot width. For modest-sized houses, that dimension meant that the garage had to lap over part of the front or be partially incorporated in some way into the body of the house itself. Since it was also preferred that garages be side-loaded, this lot type presented a particular challenge. To solve this conundrum, I first studied the prairie lots and their setbacks. Since the homesites were clustered, I grouped my farmsteads with zero lot lines, a strategy that eliminated a side-yard setback on one side and thereby allowed me to attach two two-car garages together to form a stable yard. The two L-shaped plans, mirrored, became a U-shape, a

unique compound that permitted wider side yards between the pairs. However, after fifteen years of litigation on the land, neither the owners nor Shaw wanted to rock the boat of setbacks previously approved by the village of Grayslake, so I had to look for other ways to handle the garage.

I sketched one small, three-bedroom house, deciding to celebrate the garage as a descendant of a small gabled stable by separating its doors, facing them to the street, and flanking them with overhanging front- and rear-entrance porches. All of the houses were eventually named after prominent individuals in Illinois. This one, the "Joice," became, in my expanded four-bedroom version, one of the largest houses in the development. It offered an optional fifth bedroom and an extended family room. The builder's review committee, I am sure, enlarged the house to offset the effects of the garage on the front facade. In its largest iteration, it became one of the first model houses to open in Prairie Crossing in the spring of 1995 and was sold by the fall.

The next design effort, which became the "Harrison," was based on a central "great room," bracketed on three sides by a den, kitchen, and entry. That cruciform plan was repeated on the second floor, where three bedrooms grouped about a center core offered three exposures. However, the first-floor shape was changed when the original den was expanded into a den plus a fourth bedroom and the kitchen doubled in size to accommodate a large breakfast room. When I first designed the house, I had thought that a central great room open to and flanked by a kitchen and den would convey an informal country feeling, as it had in other country houses I had done. It took this one some time to catch on, however, perhaps because of the garage that lapped a part of the front facade in a very un-farmhouse-like fashion. But somebody out there

JOICE HOUSE

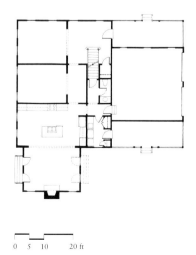

0   5   10   20 ft

HARRISON HOUSE (TWO VERSIONS)

0 5 10   20 ft

liked it, because construction finally began in 1997.

I was rapidly memorizing all the standard minimums for room sizes and their nomenclatures, as well as certain essentials that were a part of every package that would be offered, such as laundry/mudrooms, ideally with windows, located off two-car garages that had access to "bonus" rooms above them. I had to keep in mind desired design guidelines such as maximizing views to the landscape from as many rooms as possible (especially from the entrance), using as much cross-ventilation as possible, and planning for front porches and rear decks. My challenges came when I was asked to change the proportions of a particular facade to eliminate windows, in places like closets, that happened to be needed to balance the composition. I always argued the pluses of such a condition by pointing out that colors of clothing were easier to match in natural light. Many times I won, but sometimes I lost these design debates. I usually succeeded when curb appeal was in question, but had less success when it was not.

After a few false starts, I tried another scheme that produced several versions of an "Ogilvie." As per the rules, the plans were of different sizes on the second floor with varying front facades. Sometimes I was amazed at where the designs began and where they ended! The Ogilvie began with a distinctly farmstead demeanor. By that time I had figured out a way to tuck the garage alongside and to fill the offset front with windows. As with the others, the Ogilvie started out as a three-bedroom in its smallest iteration. But as our designs were rendered and sent to the sales office on the site, it became apparent that many buyers preferred the four-bedroom options. These potential purchasers, it seemed, were also prepared to select the smaller, more open plans, forgoing extra space in order to afford to buy into the development. (The energy-saving features and quality materials used in Prairie Crossing houses put them in a higher per-square-foot cost category than the competition down the road.) After the first year, I petitioned Shaw to allow me to redesign the Ogilvie to be more competitive. The four-bedroom Ogilvie II has since attracted several owners.

It was the littlest house in the development, the "Halsey," that became one of the biggest sellers. As George and Vicky Ranney analyzed the first crop of houses we designed, they realized that all of our initial designs had become inflated for one reason or another and none were available for under $200,000. Since a goal of the community had been diversity, they needed a smaller house. Frank Martin asked me to design one for the Village lots that would not only fall into a lower price category but would be less than 1,500 square feet. When a two-story house is to be that small with a bare-bones budget, a box shape is the best solution. I organized the top floor first, a flight of stairs with three bed-rooms and two baths forming a pin-wheel around it. This set the propor-tions for the floor below, where one quadrant offered two different entrances on two different sides of the house with two different porches. The remaining L-shaped space opened living room to dining room to kitchen in a flexible arrangement that appealed to young buyers. The facade was carefully and symmetri-cally organized on all four sides. Even the fireplace stood like a sen-tinel in the center of one facade, in spite of the fact that it straddled two rooms—a slight aberration from the builder norm that took some per-suading to achieve.

My last house in the series to date is the "Addams," after Jane Addams of Chicago's Hull House. It was to be a larger version of the Halsey, adding a fourth bedroom and reintroducing the family room.

OGILVIE HOUSE

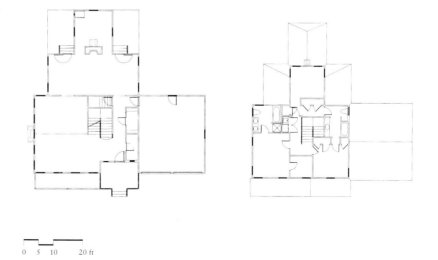

0   5   10   20 ft

HALSEY HOUSE

0   5   10   20 ft

It was also to be offered on the Prairie and Meadow lots; therefore, no placement of the garage at the rear was possible. This time I incorporated one-half of the garage into the house itself, wrapping the kitchen around it. With the exception of the eccentric garage, the basis of the design was the traditional foursquare house that has been built across America for centuries. The Addams became a spec house two years after its inception.

Marketing strategies continue to evolve as Prairie Crossing strives to prove that a conservation community can also be a profitable business venture that will recoup investments and prove to other developers across the country that stewardship of the environment and conservation of energy are viable strategies for their own developments. These last few years I have watched Prairie Crossing slowly evolve into a community. The railroads have built a station at the crossing. Its members have participated in a barn raising that reconstructed the timbers of an 1880s dairy barn into a community center. The residents have joined the Liberty Prairie Conservancy and planted community garden plots. Our friend the late Bill Turnbull, Vicky's cousin, contributed a design for the gazebo at the entrance, and I came up with a drawing for a children's playhouse. The *Prairie Crossing Gazette,* printed on recycled paper, is in everyone's mailbox, chronicling life in a community that began as a development and has since become a neighborhood. One Christmas I received a card depicting an old-fashioned snowbound village with an inscription that for me is unforgettable:

Dear Margaret,
    Thanks for all you've brought to Prairie Crossing, from the Halsey to the playhouse, from the fight for principles to the peace of symmetry.
        —Vicky and George

ADDAMS HOUSE

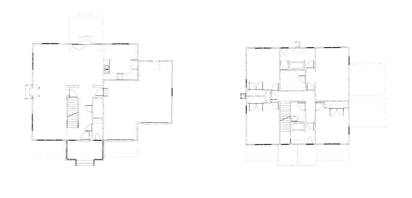

0   5   10   20 ft

MICHIGAN SHORES CLUB

Wilmette, Illinois
1992–99

Designed in 1928 in the English Tudor style by D. H. Burnham and Company (actually the descendants, Hubert and Daniel Jr., of Daniel H. Burnham), and originally named the Shawnee Country Club, this building was constructed on a bluff overlooking Lake Michigan in the village of Wilmette, a suburb on Chicago's North Shore. The club faced directly onto the lake and hosted many memorable galas when members spilled out of the dining room onto the upper terrace to gaze at the waves breaking on the beach below. In the depths of the Great Depression the club sold the land below the bluff to the village for a water-treatment plant, and the terrace lost its appeal, subse-

quently and rather expediently becoming an enclosed porch. Other less than sympathetic remodelings followed suit in the ensuing years, as rooms were adapted to new functions. The historic character of the club slowly eroded.

We were retained by the board in 1992 to prepare a master plan for the renovation of all areas of the club that had been "modernized" over the past fifty years. We developed a phased and budgeted long-range plan for architectural restoration and remodeling that included interior furnishings. We began the work with the revenue-producing rooms, namely those ceremonial chambers often reserved for weddings and banquets. Two-thirds of the

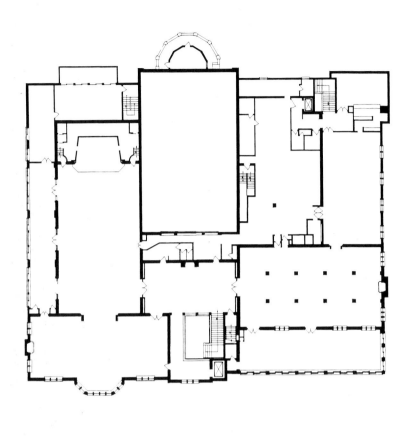

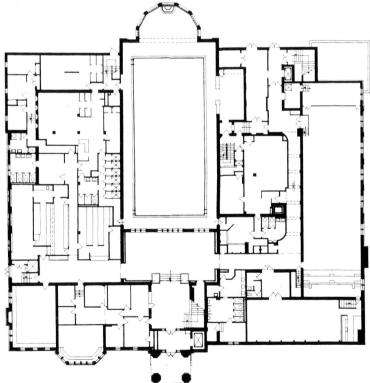

0   10   20   40 ft

plan was completed by 1997, the last of the public dining rooms and corridors will be complete in 1999.

Phase I removed the low-ceilinged upper porch. A new limestone-clad one was designed, with tall windows commensurate with the transomed ones opening into the dining room beyond. Dropped soffits designed as timbered rafters conceal supply ducts, while leaded-glass doors add authenticity. The dining room itself required reduction rather than remodeling. The acoustic-tile ceiling, mirrored column covers, and fireplace overmantel were removed, revealing the elegantly proportioned room underneath that was then

changed by a subdued color scheme and new fixtures. These same reductive measures were applied to other rooms on the second floor, where a judicious paint selection enhanced existing Burnhamesque detailing.

Phase IB tackled the front lobby, removing all traces of the 1960s modernization such as the metal stair railing. New wooden railings based on the original Burnham designs were carved, and limestone-colored paint articulated the plaster tracery and concrete beams. What Jacobean-style furniture the club possessed was restored and reupholstered, and new pieces were purchased at antiques auctions to supplement the collection.

Lounge seating was selected to approximate high-backed settees of the period; new carpeting was woven in England, and wrought-iron-and-stone tables, as well as lights and accessories, were specified. Stone benches under the windows welcomed children.

Perhaps the most dramatic transformation was wrought in the rear corridor. Cut through the men's locker room in the distant past, it was created to link a rear-entry addition and parking lot to the front of the club. Since D. H. Burnham and Company never designed this corridor, the architects or contractors of the 1960s expressed themselves in the style of the day. By

the time the engineers dropped the ceiling to conceal air-conditioning systems squeezed into the concrete structure, the passageway used by most club members had become a descent into purgatory. We shoved some protruding lockers back into the locker room to straighten one portion of the corridor and then detailed faux-stone-cased openings at each jog in the corridor or break in the ceiling or floor plane (the passage dropped over a foot from rear to front). Each doorway along the route was symmetrically framed. Gothic windows glazed in milk glass were cut into interior walls to borrow light from the bowling alley. A new display case was designed at the terminus of the western leg to house bowling trophies, and wooden french doors replaced their aluminum counterparts. Multi-hued slate flooring inlaid at the rear protected the entrance while offering certain authenticity.

In Phase II we completed the medievalization of the rear addition. We covered the modern brick walls enclosing the stairway that leads up to the Oak Room on the second floor in plaster, painted as stone. This casual dining room had been the original practice putting green until a bar was stuck onto its rear. The concrete stair configuration was obviously fixed, but we were able to replace the fake planter bed with a fake cloister, complete with a trompe l'oeil landscape visible through its Gothic arches. By relocating the doors into the Oak Room we were able to achieve not only symmetry in the dining room but an actual landing at the top of the stairs. The room was then repainted and refurbished. Last, the bar itself was reconfigured to increase the service capabilities and storage capacities while improving its appearance.

There remain but a few public areas at the south end of the club that have yet to be medievalized, but our restorative spirits are undaunted. Old Daniel Burnham has undoubtedly ceased rolling over quite as frequently in his grave.

WILDWOOD

Bridgman, Michigan
1993–94

Michiana sand dunes are magic mountains. In this area near the Michigan-Indiana border, the prevailing westerly winds blow across Lake Michigan, piling the sand up in great mounds against the lake's southeastern shore. It is sand so fine that it squeaks when one walks across it, stopped in its constant shifting only by dune grasses and horsetail ferns, which form sharp-edged clumps. The Indiana Dunes National Lake Shore first captivated our family when we lived on the South Side of Chicago, less than an hour's drive from them. As children, my siblings and I spent many summer weekends alternately dodging waves, prancing along the sand bars, or building up sandcastles at the water's edge.

Then for two consecutive summers when I was nine and ten, I was shipped off for a week to a generic church camp another thirty miles up the coast in Bridgman, where the Warren Dunes formed tall bluffs along the shore. The camp's white-washed frame buildings were clustered in the woods, facing onto a large "blow out" in the dunes. After dinner, we were allowed to participate in our favorite pastime of swinging on a rope that was attached to a sturdy oak limb reaching far out over that wind-swept depression. Letting go at the top of the arc, we flew through the air, landing on the soft sand below. Nothing in the way of biblical teaching left as strong an impression on me as did the camp itself with its sturdy clapboard buildings settled into vast acres of rolling dunes.

When Stanley and I first built Boardwalk ten miles to the south of Bridgman, I made a pilgrimage back to the old camp, only to find the long dirt road that led back into the sand dunes from the Red Arrow Highway overgrown and the buildings boarded up. Even the "blow out" had been filled in with sand. About the time we found our prop-

erty in Lakeside, a developer bought a large portion of those wooded dunes near the old Bridgman camp and called his project Wildwood. He subdivided the land into five-acre sites that sold very slowly over the ensuing ten years, in part because of the extreme isolation of the parcel. One of those five-acre sites was purchased by our friends Judith and Julius in 1993.

We had met this couple in the early 1980s during those Bloomsburgian weekends at our friend Rhona's rental cottage in Sawyer. Charmed by the area these two historians—one a professor of medieval Italian history and the other a professor, curator, and critic of contemporary art—searched for their own weekend retreat in Harbor Country. In 1984, they found a small, unheated cottage on Forest Road in a section of Harbert called Spring Brook. Judith and I had ridden our bicycles along the back country lanes that branched off Prairie Road, the access to Spring Brook as well as to several other small enclaves, each with its own communal beach. On one such excursion, we rode into the neighboring Prairie Club, founded in the 1910s by a group of intellectuals led by Carl Sandburg. His white frame house was perched with others side-by-side on one of the wooded hills overlooking the lake.

While Spring Brook did not have the cachet of its more illustrious neighbor, it did have a number of older frame cottages set down on its sandy soil among sturdy oaks and tall pines. The cottage Judith and Julius bought was a modest, two-bedroom, single-bath frame structure built in the 1920s. Wedged between two others on a small lot, Judith referred to it as "the shack" when she asked me to winterize it and expand it into three bedrooms to better suit their family, which included a teenage son and daughter. Working within their budget, I converted the miniature living/dining room into the

master bedroom, adding a second bath and a desk set under a window between two curtained closets. The old small screened entry/porch became their private retreat as I added a new, larger porch and adjoining family room off the rear, reconfiguring the adjacent kitchen in the process.

The little blue rehab became more and more used as other Chicago friends found similar properties in nearby towns. Judith during this time kept tabs on the construction of Wit's End, which was several miles away

medieval towers of San Gimignano, whose fortifications have inspired architects for centuries. Although the beach was to be found over yet another hill, and no matter how high we built a tower the water still couldn't be seen, the idea of such a structure in the trees was very appealing. So we sat down to discuss a program that might produce such a building. Research indicated that Lake Township's residential zoning laws permitted only a height of thirty feet at the midpoint of the roof; and a three-story house had to

by car, but only a short distance as the crow flies across a few acres of blueberry fields. Six years later, she found a five-acre lot in Wildwood, which happened to be across the road from another couple who were mutual friends. In the early spring of 1993, we hiked up Judith's wooded hill searching for the ideal setting for the new house.

Judith and Julius had returned the previous year from a sabbatical in Italy. As we reminisced about Tuscany, we especially recalled the many

have half of the lower story buried in the ground. This last restriction would not be a problem, since we would be building on a hillside facing a small clearing. We then decided on several things: the children were old enough to occupy the ground floor with two bedrooms and a shared bath; the entrance, family room, and kitchen would be located on the middle level along with the all-important screened porch; and the parent's bedroom, study, and bath would be situated on the third

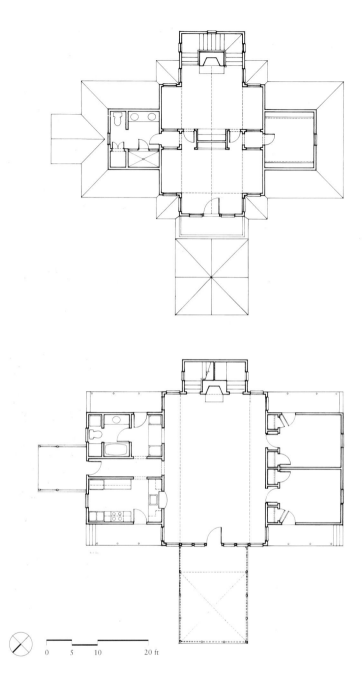

0   5   10   20 ft

These two rooms are, in turn, paired by their counterparts, the children's bedrooms. Four decks are included, one off each room; each child has his or her own outdoor space. The mudroom has a secondary entrance off of it, and the kitchen has a place for Julius's grill and Judith's collection of potted herbs.

We discussed important issues about the house, one of which was its relationship with the environment. We wondered how breezes and cross-breezes would blow through the rooms and how sunlight would play across surfaces. The balance between openness to the woods and wildlife and the sense of security achieved with closure was also a concern. The family room, which is both the literal and figurative center of the house, becomes that fulcrum as it sets up a second cross-axis, focusing on the hearth at one end of the room, an almost cavelike condition that is countered by the transparency of the other end, which opens onto the screened porch. This is a totally transparent space that is in turn counterbalanced by the regularity of the wooden grid that contains and separates it from the irregularities of nature. A tighter grid then screens a storage area below the porch. Each of the four corners of this central room is glazed so that the sun's rays penetrate into some part of the room at every time of the day. After the family moved into the house, Judith reported that one winter afternoon, as she was reading by the fire, she watched a deer completely circum-navigate the house.

Encircling the fireplace, the stairway rises up to the parental quarters on the second floor, designed as a place of study and repose. Since the stair tower, like the porch, is an asymmetrical addition to an otherwise symmetrical scheme, it too is gridded on the exterior facades by batons covering marine plywood, much like Boardwalk's two ends. Small square windows are placed

level. But try as I might, I could not make the three floors stack up properly. The middle floor had too many square feet—it bulged out over the lower level, and budget concerns demanded easy-to-construct shapes. Thus the tower was abandoned.

The two-story scheme proved equally challenging. All the pieces had to fall into place within 2,200 square feet. Proceeding from the entrance, the plan became cruciate, which placed the main gathering space in the center, where it would act as a pivot point. However, in this scheme, one reaches the center after entering into a hallway flanked by the kitchen on one side and a mudroom with adjoining bath on the other. Both rooms are entered at the cross-axis, where opposing french doors frame the landscape. Both rooms also have symmetrically paired "windows" opening onto the family room, extending the space visually and encouraging sociability.

within the grid to light the stair and inglenook. The plan of this level is also cruciate. The couple's quarters overlook the front and rear, and from their upper deck, one can peer down through the open gable into the interior of the porch below. The suite echoes, in square footage, the family room below, but the small flanking bath and dressing rooms are stepped back, their forms emerging from the hipped roofs that surround them.

We decided that as a reflection of the couple's joint aesthetic, the house should take its clues from the Midwestern vernacular, and we agreed that it should reinterpret that tradition to create a form both familiar and a little foreign. Although it might use a well-known architectural vocabulary, it would reassemble and reproportion common components in order to speak its own contemporary language. This transformation of conventional forms into new ones that defer to precedent without becoming slaves to it is one of the guiding principles behind my practice.

In Wildwood, one variation of a traditional architectural language is the use of the abstract grid, a device that connotes measurement and thereby is a method establishing order and scale. This results in the achievement of a certain tranquillity that evolves from the resolution of spatial relationships in a harmonious manner. What links Wildwood to its predecessors in other centuries is a certain formality of plan and composition, an austerity of form rooted in function. It could be either the quintessential cottage or a one-room schoolhouse, farmhouse, or camp cabin. It is not precisely any of these, yet it is a synthesis of all of them. It refers to a time of frugality of form and materials. Built in the middle of a recession that many architects preferred to call a depression, it is both a reaffirmation of the act of construction and a reintroduction to the art of conservation.

McCLINTOCK CAMP

Grand Marais, Michigan
1994–96

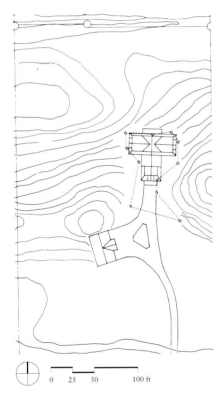

```
        0   25   50        100 ft
```

Doug gave me to Janet for her birthday. It was just before the holidays in 1993 that the couple came to Chicago to interview Stanley and me. It soon became apparent that their predilections were for a house that responded to regional characteristics. The couple lived in a suburb of Detroit and were in the process of purchasing ten acres of wooded duneland in a subdivision on the shore of Lake Superior in Michigan's Upper Peninsula. Their property in Grand Marais, a small resort community, was a two-hour drive eastward along the coast from the first McClintock family hunting-and-fishing camp, which was near Marquette. Janet is an interior designer who specializes in library design, and Doug has an accounting position with Arthur Andersen. They took related roles in the design process, with Janet intimately involved in the design decisions and Doug concerned with management and budget.

We discussed the feasibility of my designing a country house, or "camp" as they would call it, from afar. I had done so in Colorado and in Massachusetts, but my clients had been fellow Chicagoans. I told them that a good contractor was a key to the success of long-distance construction. We would need to find one in that remote part of the country who was quite competent but not so independent that he or she would be unwilling to work with an architect. As far as our own long-distance relationship was concerned, once we had agreed upon a program—which could be assembled during a reconnaissance visit to the Upper Peninsula to inspect the site and interview contractors—I would then plan to meet with them shortly thereafter to present the preliminary schematic designs. If the concept was approved, my office could proceed to develop a set of working drawings. Janet was prepared to be the interior designer on the project and to make all the furniture, furnishings, and equipment selections. We would then assemble before the drawings were complete to review finishes, lighting layouts, and electrical and mechanical drawings. Aiming for the absolute minimum number of site visits, we discussed a second trip when the house was framed and a final one when the project was substantially complete. Before they returned to Detroit, we arranged to meet in the late spring in Lakeside so that they could see Boardwalk, Wit's End, and Wildwood. Since their property was already engulfed in snow, it made sense to wait until spring for the initial visit.

Four months later, on the first of May, the couple drove the three or more hours required to cross Michigan laterally and arrived in Lakeside in time for Sunday brunch. After the house tours, we discussed a time schedule for proceeding with the work and a potential budget based on the cost-per-square-foot of a current project. I explained that $115-per-square-foot should be considered the bare minimum for a modest building.

We also discussed our need for a topographic survey of the property. When they showed me the plot plan and the photographs they had taken of the wooded site, it was apparent that to see the water, the house needed to be as close to the shore as the so-called Critical Dunes Act would allow. That act states that, for all property that abuts any undeveloped shoreline in the state of Michigan, the Department of National Resources (DNR) needs to approve the siting of any proposed structures. The rule is that the structure must be set back one hundred feet from the crest of the primary dune and no foundation can be set into a dune that has a slope of 25 percent or greater.

We settled on a date in late May to meet in Marquette, Michigan, and drive the seventy-five miles to Grand Marais. I was scheduled to supervise

the photography of the Lighthouse on Martha's Vineyard over Memorial Day weekend and planned to fly from there to Marquette, arriving late on Tuesday and connecting with my clients the following day. Summer had come to the Vineyard, but not to the Upper Peninsula. The skies were leaden and the wind blew straight from Ontario, Canada, as we drove through Marquette's small historic district in search of regional characteristics, of which there were surprisingly few. Some substantial public buildings were built of a local sandstone, but many private homes were of frame construction not unlike many middle-class Chicago suburbs. So we proceeded to Grand Marais, stopping midway to interview an eccentric woodworker in Munising who had been recommended to Janet as a possible contractor.

During the drive, we discussed their program. Janet had prepared an outline and I reviewed room types, sizes, and relationships and the fact that as many of them as possible should face the lake even though that exposure was due north. Within 2,000 to 2,400 square feet, not counting an exterior deck, the main building was to contain, on the main level, a great room with a high ceiling and a stone fireplace, as well as storage for books and games; an adjacent office alcove for Doug; an adjacent porch or sunroom with separate egress; and a kitchen open to everyday dining. The master bedroom and bath would also occupy this level, preferably in a "quiet zone" with no rooms above. And last, there was to be a substantial mudroom with an air lock and benches and also a small laundry. The upper level would contain two children's rooms with one bath and the lower level a walk-out basement. A detached garage would house two cars and a boat; the garage might have a studio and guest quarters above.

The property was actually part of a newly plotted subdivision on the outskirts of Grand Marais. The developer of the complex, called Superior Dunes, had laid out the lots side by side as a series of long rectangles, with each parcel having two hundred feet of lake frontage on the short side and a total area of ten acres. Dune Road, the access through the subdivision, bisected each parcel, but the Superior Dunes association bylaws did not permit building a secondary residence on the inboard five acres for a period of five years after purchase, so in effect this acreage actually appeared to be a part of the forest. We stopped along the side of the road between the markers that indicated lot number seven and opened the car doors. The air was as crisp and clear, the pine trees as redolent of resin, as they can be only this deep in the north woods. As we tramped back through the forest toward the lake, the ground was springy underfoot with pine needles, and the intermittent boulders we circumvented were covered in lichen.

I had sent ahead of me a topographic model of the site constructed from the edge of the lake to a point behind the highest hill. We intended to locate on the model the optimal site for the camp, based on our observation of the actual terrain and sight lines through the trees to the lake. The association rules allowed only 25 percent of the trees on one's property to be removed or thinned out, and since the house itself would account for some of them, we needed to be circumspect in selecting others for removal. Our model was prepared from a topographical map provided by the developer, and we had determined where the slopes in excess of 25 percent fell. Standing on the ridge in a slight depression between two flanking hills, we looked far down the slope through the trees to the lake; its edge began at the edge of the forest without any sandy strip of beach. In spite of the wind, the lake was still. We crisscrossed the site just below the top of

the hill, making sure that we were one hundred feet back from the water's edge. This edge, we had been assured, constituted the dune crest. We selected a shallow spot with an open glade where we could angle the camp to the northwest, so that its long dimension would be parallel to the contours of the land, which would slope naturally away from it down to the shore.

After recording our site selection on the model, we departed to Grand Marais for the night. The next morning, we inspected work being done by a local builder that was under construction in town. Noting the popcorn ceilings and prefabricated plywood siding, we decided that we would have to go farther afield to find the quality of workmanship we all wanted. The couple's wish list included low-maintenance but costly items such as Pella windows; a standing-seam metal roof; stone, slate, or wood floors; a stone chimney; and cherry wainscoting and/or

ceilings. The association's protective covenants listed deed restrictions that mandated the use of stained cedar shingles or clapboard on 75 percent of the exterior and a roof pitch on the main structure of at least eight-in-twelve. They also included the phrase: "Any structure erected on the parcel shall be finished in such a manner as shall be compatible with surrounding structures."

We returned to Marquette to interview additional contractors and inspect their workmanship, selecting one who said that he actually preferred to work from a complete set of architectural plans and had no problem in deferring to the architect for all design decisions. At the time, Gary was running a job in Florida for an acquaintance of mine on the Committee on Design and driving back and forth every other weekend. We thought he was a little crazy, but he didn't seem to mind the commute. Gary said he would plan to bring a framing crew to Grand Marais from

Marquette to work during the week and return them home on the weekends. He agreed to assist with any negotiations with the DNR and to review our plans in progress to assure us that they were within the budget parameters. However, he was adamant that a figure under $100-per-square-foot was not unreasonable. I was very skeptical and reminded the couple of our cost estimates, but labor was supposed to be cheaper in northern Michigan.

Nevertheless, I quickly prepared preliminary sketches to present to Janet when she came to Chicago in the middle of June for Neocon, the contract-design industry's annual exposition. The plans I sketched stretched out her program in an eighty-five-foot-long lake-facing line from the sunroom on the west to the master bedroom on the east. The double-height great room occupied dead center and was flanked by a kitchen and dining room and backed by a mudroom entry and stair tower. The children's rooms sat above the kitchen and dining room looking over a balcony to the great room below. With minor adjustments, the plans were approved, and we began to prepare elevations so that in early July Janet could take a full set of plans before the association's review board. They passed, and in preparation for the end-of-summer visit by the DNR, we sent off a detailed site plan to Gary, who staked out the camp's footprint in the area we had designated.

Then the boom fell. As Gary reported, the DNR representative looked at our stakes and decided that some were set in slopes of greater than 25 percent. He told Gary that after years of experience he could "eyeball" such conditions. Without recourse to measuring devices, he drew on our site plan, instead of our footprint, an amoeba-shaped form that he called the area of impact. It was only sixty-five feet wide at its irregularly

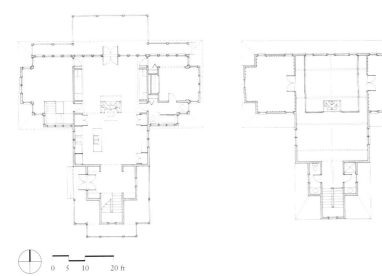

0   5   10   20 ft

151

required that the adjacent soil be shored up during construction. For Gary's crew to even pour a foundation meant that a trench several feet wider than the actual foundation wall needed to be dug by hand so that the formwork could be placed for the wall and the footings. It took a month to put the foundation plans together. In the process, the full basement shrank to comply with DNR-designated depths that could be dug into the dune. It was located only in the northwest corner of the foundation where the contours were lowest; the remaining area became crawl space. This condition also necessitated placing a second stair in this section that accessed the basement, so we tucked it into a corner of the sunroom and moved the laundry to the lower level. With all of the stepping of the plan required to navigate within the amoeba's shape, the camp's image took on an interesting character. We made a special model of the camp and a container to hold it, which Doug put under the Christmas tree for Janet in December of 1994.

We met in Chicago immediately after the first of the year to finalize the finishes, select hardware, and review the electrical and plumbing plans. We proceeded to complete the plans and specifications, presenting them to Gary to price the following month. The second boom then dropped for Janet and Doug. The $100-per-square-foot figure was indeed unrealistic. We knew that the intricate foundation work would add approximately $25,000 to the job, and I had reminded the couple that there were costs associated with many windows and many setbacks, but the necessary complexities of the plans coupled with the fine finishes added even more to the square-foot price than was anticipated. Once again, we needed to reduce the scope of the camp.

To optimize views of the lake and the amount of available light that

shaped widest point and was no longer parallel to the contour lines, instead running across them. This meant that the camp's lake facade would face due north, but that the land would slope down across this facade from east to west, and the structure would no longer sit on the site with a sympathetic relationship to the hillside. There appeared to be no recourse or appeal; the DNR's decision was final. We were forced to redesign the project to fit these arbitrary boundaries.

We came up with a new scheme that stepped the kitchen and dining room to the rear behind the great room and stepped the entry stair

back yet again, in a symmetrical progression that appeared to work within the amoeba. But we were taking no chances. We asked the DNR representative to stake the site so that we could have an accurate survey made by connecting the dots of his stakes and dimensioning them. Janet and Doug needed to be assured that the remaining scaled-down room sizes were adequate for their needs. We also hired a local engineer to design the foundations because of the many stepbacks needed to squeeze rectangular rooms into an amorphous form and because the DNR decreed that any part of the foundation that came near the impact line

filtered through the trees, we had used transoms over windows and doors and a ceiling height of ten feet on the first floor. Our first adjustment was to eliminate all the transoms and drop the ceiling down to nine feet on the main level and eight feet on the second level. We discussed eliminating the two stories worth of stone from the fireplace, but this would have seriously diminished the camplike quality of the main room. What we did alter in this room were the specially designed fir fan trusses. The standing-seam metal roof was replaced with an asphalt shingle one. We used the same red shingles as Wild-

wood, which, coupled with the forest-green stain on the clapboard siding, gave the camp a more casual air—one more in keeping with the ad hoc aura of the spartan camps of yesteryear. Janet kept her cherry wainscoting but gave up her painting studio over the garage.

Once the numbers were adjusted, construction began in late spring of 1995 when the last snow had melted. Our project architect approved the framing in late June, and before the snows fell again in the fall the house was roofed and sided and closed in for the winter. During the construction process, which Janet and Doug were super-

vising, Gary declared bankruptcy. Doug took over the administration of the contracts, communicating with the subcontractors directly. He hired the first woodworker we had interviewed in Munising to supervise the completion of the interior finishing, and the couple hung up Mackinaws and spread out Hudson Bay blankets on the beds a year after construction began. Joking about the trials and tribulations of the building process with Janet after the dust had settled and they had had a season to themselves at the camp, I was tempted to ask her if she had ever seen the movie "Mr. Blandings Builds His Dream House."

NEISSER CONDOMINIUM

Chicago, Illinois
1994–96

It is sad to reflect on the fact that sometimes projects occur as the result of tragic circumstances. What brought Stanley and me together on a project for the first time since the Chicago Bar Association was the death of one of his closest friends. It was a friendship that began during college and was reinforced later in Lakeside when Edward and Judith Neisser rented the guest cottage at the Dormers, the former lake estate of one of Chicago's founding families, now owned by mutual friends. Judy's preference was for intellectual pursuits, preferably pursued indoors, but Ed, an outdoorsman, often teamed up with Rhona, one of Judy's oldest friends, to take us on in rotating doubles matches with the estate owners on their tennis court, which abutted their patch of Midwestern prairie.

Judy was a consummate hostess, as well as a freelance writer. Often contributing stories to the shelter magazines, she had written the article about the Nineteenth-Century Farmhouse for *Architectural Digest*'s "before and after" issue. In her hostess role, she often organized familial dinner parties at the cottage for the Harbor Country crowd.

During the summer of 1991 several tragedies occurred, on an epic scale, that were to transform Judy's world. The couple's son, David, an investment banker, was struck down by a speeding car, suffering permanent brain damage and requiring institutional care. Ed was diagnosed with a rare form of lung cancer. He fought courageously for a year and a half, succumbing in June 1993, shortly after the marriage of their daughter, Kate, a school psychologist and writer. The following spring Judy searched for new surroundings that would also be accessible for David, who was bound to a wheelchair. She found in Streeterville, two blocks from Stanley's and my apartment, an unbuilt 4,400-square-foot condominium on the sixty-second

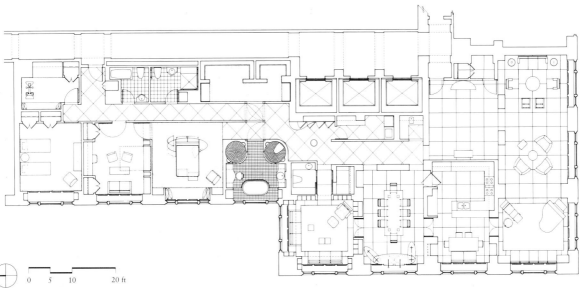

floor of Kohn Pedersen Fox's new complex at the end of the Magnificent Mile, which also housed a hotel and a large shopping mall. Judy sold her Lincoln Park town house shortly thereafter and immediately moved into the hotel.

The raw space she had located looked like anything but a piece of cake to cut up when Stanley and I were called over to see it. Although the ceilings were an exciting twelve and a half feet, another owner and his architect had produced some preliminary plans that had unfortunately proceeded to the extent of installing a potpourri of plumbing pipes to support numerous planned water features. All this we learned as Judy, standing in the new space, announced that Stanley and I together were going to be her architects and she would brook no arguments. While we did not collaborate that often, this time we made an exception.

Once we had assembled and digested all the building restrictions that an active condominium association could invent, it was time to begin. Stanley immediately took pencil to paper. Judy's favorite building was Pierre Chareau's Maison de Verre in Paris, and she had a vision that her own space might assume certain of its industrial aesthetics.

She was a minimalist and a modernist, as Ed had been, and their eclectic furniture collection ran the gamut from the Italian and American art deco of the 1930s through the Bauhaus masters and into the 1950s with the work of Charles and Ray Eames. Occasionally, an African stool or a bench by the artist Jenny Holzer joined the mix. These modernist sensibilities were also reflected in her contemporary-art collection, assembled in part with Rhona's assistance.

Judy's first thoughts were of a loftlike space, but in the end she reached the conclusion that she preferred the sense of enclosure that rooms provide. This coincided with the completion of our analysis of the plumbing situation, wherein we concluded that walls were necessary to enclose and conceal the plethora of pipes. Judy had actually purchased two apartments, and each had its own set of plumbing risers, dictating where bathrooms and kitchen could occur. We planned to raise the finished floor four inches to conceal the rerouting of any small pipes that could be manipulated, but we also needed to core the concrete floor to relocate the larger ones, and each coring required approval by the

condo board. Some eight-inch waste stacks could not be rerouted but could be bent over into elbows that became encased in artistically delineated low walls. Even fixed electrical panel boxes needed to be accommodated and concealed. It took days and the involvement of several engineers to document all the obstacles before we could draw them on the plans and determine how to deal with them as well as how to work within the column bays.

Although Stanley's work and my work have evolved in differing ways, the influence of modernism and the Miesian tradition has always been

present, sometimes just below the surface, sometimes above. We are equally drawn to classical symmetries, having absorbed them into our psyches the months we lived in Rome and the years we studied the Renaissance masters. Stanley sometimes begins with symmetry, only to set up oppositions to it when he is exploring theoretical positions. My own use of symmetry is more overt. I find that its ordering principles create a sense of balance in a space that form a tranquil place. Certainly what we wanted for Judy was a place that would, by its very presence, provide a sanctuary where she could pick up the threads of her life and begin to heal the emotional wounds left by the loss of half her family.

This new place was also intended to provide a setting in which she could entertain great numbers of her friends. To that end, we identified a series of rooms required for different functions. We needed to create a reasonably sized foyer with guest closet, and since the front-door location was set by the layout of the condominium corridors, we needed to organize the detailing of the entrance to balance its asymmetrical condition. This would be the only internal room of import. All other rooms would partake of the sweeping views of the city to the north, south, and west. The living room needed to accommodate her Warren McArthur collection as well as a grouping of Italian deco lounge chairs. Connected to the living room, a music room with space for a grand piano was required. Judy's son-in-law, Stephen, was a concert trumpet player and music professor, and she wanted a place for him to practice with an accompanist or perform when he came to visit. The kitchen location was established by the plumbing, but it needed a breakfast room as well. Adjacent to it, the dining room needed to accommodate Judy's special glass-topped table, one in an artist's series. Each bronze leg

windows that Kohn Pedersen Fox proportioned after the classic "Chicago window" of the Chicago school are raised some two feet above the floor. I felt strongly that our design aesthetic needed to acknowledge and address this condition and turn it from a minus into a plus. This system, a smaller version of a radiator, posed a detailing problem because even when the units were boxed out to the column edge and set just below the window frame to form a continuous window seat, air needed to flow into them from below and out from above. While the building as a whole is a postmodern structure clad in French limestone, the windows are purely modern. Setting each window bay into a shadow box formed by the columns at its side, the soffit above, and the window seat below, caused it to be read as a deep recess. We decided to detail a scored flush wooden base for all the walls at the same two-foot height as the window seats, establishing a datum line, and selected a Portuguese limestone for the floors in the public areas akin to the building's exterior; thus the interior would be successfully and purposefully integrated with the exterior.

Our intention to create a melding of classicism and modernism was carried through in the nine-foot-tall classically inspired french doors; their bottom rail falls at the same datum line of the window seats. This registration is repeated in the library bookcases, which are set into the window poché. These doors express the axis that connects one public room to the next in a classical enfilade. Even the bathroom and bedroom doors are french, although the glass is laminated for privacy. The detailing is minimal and modern. The reveal, a classic contemporary device for separating differing materials or delineating surfaces, is used throughout as a design strategy that is an integral part of a classical parti. Paul Goldberger, in an article

was formed as an extruded letter; together they spelled out "Think." A much-used room would be the library, since it would also serve as an informal place to gather for cocktails before dinner. Last, besides the usual service areas of laundry, storage, bar, and bathrooms, there needed to be three bedrooms: a master bedroom, an adjacent one serving also as Judy's study, and a final one for guests. And everything needed to be wheelchair-accessible.

Within the parameters set by column grid, window bay, and plumbing riser, Stanley set out to develop a plan for the rooms that organized them in a classical procession start-ing at the low-ceilinged entrance. This room was placed in a basic column bay, to which we added a second column, furred out and encased in drywall, to create a symmetrical colonnade through which one passes into the living room, which occupies two column bays, and then into the music room, which fills a third. As we did in all the other perimeter rooms with their tall ceilings, we dropped a soffit to the top of the windows to contain the air-conditioning and lighting systems. The heating system is a fan-coil unit that runs in a continuous strip along a concrete beam beneath each window. For this reason the tripartite aluminum-clad

written for *Architectural Digest*, summed up our intentions: "In the Neisser apartment, modernism feels not like an oppositional force to classicism, but like a partner to it. Traditional, highly articulated space is married to detail of rare precision and restraint and the result is both exhilarating and serene."

It is difficult to determine which of us was responsible for what in the design of the apartment, except that Stanley produced the first plan, and as the project neared completion our marriage and the partnership seemed to be surviving all the stress and strains of the collaboration.

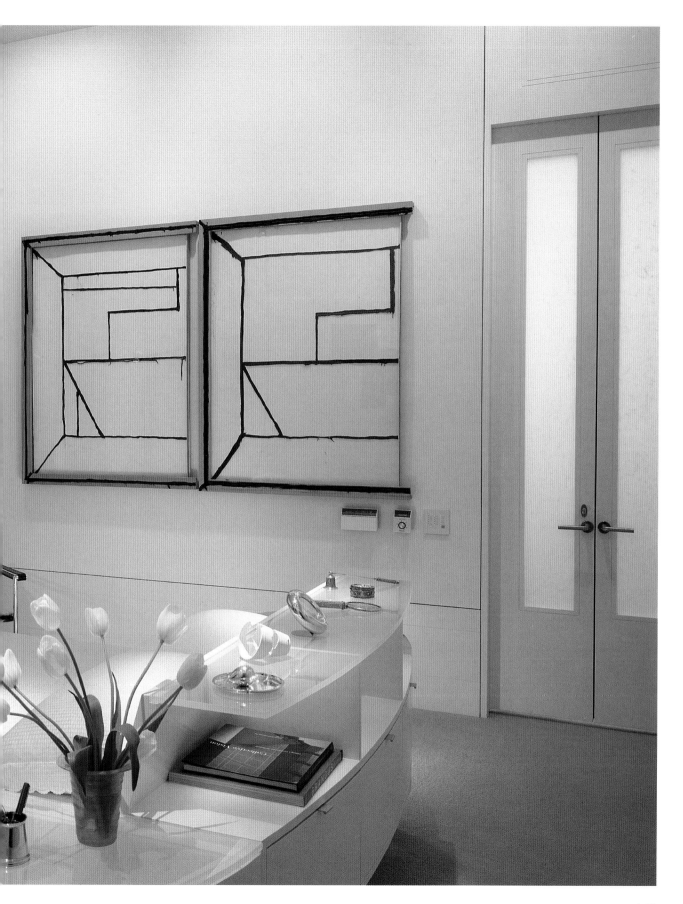

NEISSER HOUSE

Aspen, Colorado
1995–97

Aspen is connected to Chicago as it is to no other city in the world, in spite of an infusion in recent years of movie stars from Los Angeles, oil barons from Houston, and socialites from New York, as well as members of the jet set from the six other continents. When I first saw it as a child in the summer of 1950, the Aspen Institute for Humanistic Studies had just been founded, and symposiums interspersed with musicales were being held under an enormous canvas tent designed by Eero Saarinen that was pitched in the Meadows on the northern edge of town. My father had heard stories of this intellectual

encampment in the valley of the Roaring Fork River from friends in the Chicago architectural community and decided on a family vacation comprised of meanderings on foot or by horseback through the Rocky Mountains combined with a modicum of culture.

It was in 1939 that Elizabeth Paepcke, a Chicago socialite and aesthete in search of a skiing adventure, first rediscovered Aspen, which was at the time a poverty-stricken, played-out, silver-mining camp. That winter, she traveled to this isolated spot deep in the Elk Mountain Range from her family's ranch on the front range, the seven-thousand-acre wildlife

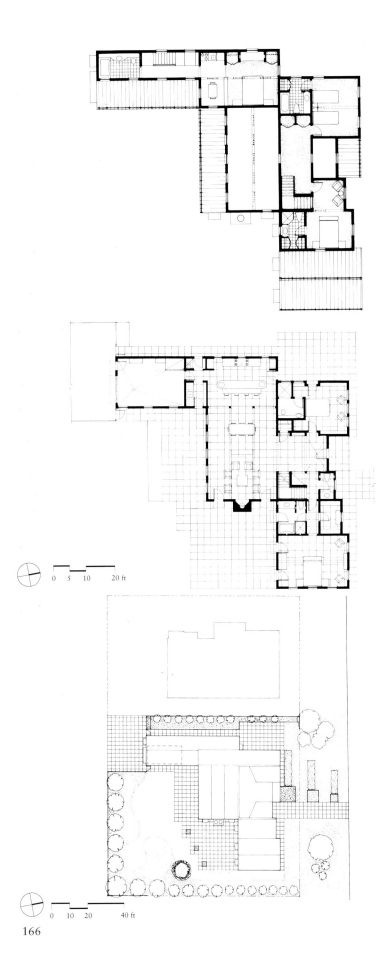

0 5 10 20 ft

0 10 20 40 ft

preserve Perry Park. She came with friends from Washington to ski on Aspen Mountain, which was riddled with ancient mining claims. They stayed at the only hotel in town, the rickety old red-stone Jerome, built in the nineteenth century at the peak of the silver boom. Riding up the backside of the mountain to the Midnight Mine with a truckload of miners, the party hiked further up the slope to Little Annie Basin and then skied down into town at the base of the mountain. Pussy Paepcke, as she had been known since childhood, did not return again to Aspen until 1946, when she brought her industrialist husband, Walter, who was the founder of Container Corporation of America.

During the war, the only activity that had disturbed the tranquillity of Aspen's few inhabitants was the training of the Army's Tenth Mountain Division, but when Walter first set eyes on this alpine valley, he immediately decided it was the ideal spot in which to create his version of a utopian community. In the clarity of the clean, mountain air one could practice the principle of developing a sound mind in a sound body as espoused by the Bauhaus and taught by his Hungarian friend László Moholy-Nagy, who had emigrated from Paris to Chicago to run the Institute of Design. This new school, founded in 1937, was intended to be an American Bauhaus and had as members of its original steering committee Walter Paepcke and architect George Fred Keck. Enlisting the support of colleagues from the University of Chicago, the Paepckes brought their guru, Walter Gropius, from Harvard. As the initiating director of the German Bauhaus in Dessau, it was he who had espoused the idea that people could enrich their lives by combining intellectual pursuits with healthy personal habits.

Herbert Bayer, a colleague of Gropius's, was hired to restore and renovate the Victorian town of

Aspen, and eventually to design the modern complex of buildings and facilities known collectively as the Aspen Institute. From the University of Chicago also came the philosopher Mortimer Adler, whose Great Books program was to form the basis for the institute's pedagogy when combined with Walter Paepcke's theories. He believed that the melding of culture with commerce could improve the quality of peoples' lives, and he sought to convince the business community to incorporate design strategy as an integral part of their organizational planning. To this end, Walter hired Skidmore, Owings & Merrill to design many of the Container Corporation's plants and offices around the country, including several in the Chicago area. I was involved in the design of the interiors of two of them as one of my first assignments when I joined SOM in 1966. Stanley also worked on Container Corporation buildings when he worked there some years before me. It was a practice in those days that all designers use the CCA's Color Harmony Manual to specify colors for all SOM projects, and we were also very influenced by their graphics program.

Although Walter died in 1960, before he could realize his final dream of having a coterie of internationally renowned architects design buildings in Aspen, Pussy maintained her status as Aspen's first lady, returning every summer to her house overlooking Hallam Lake in the West End until her death there thirty-four years later. She lived around the corner from Stanley and me on Lake Shore Drive and we sometimes saw her tall, elegant figure accompanied by her equally elegant friend John Entenza stroll by us on the way to afternoon tea at the nearby Casino Club. John was the director of the Graham Foundation and became one of Stanley's friends and mentors when, as editor, he first published Stanley's work in his *Arts & Architecture* magazine in

August of 1958. Two months before Pussy Paepcke died, I was able to tell her that she had won the prestigious Design for Humanity Award given annually by the American Society of Interior Designers for her lifelong commitment to the Aspen Institute, which included the International Design Conference as well as the Center for Environmental Studies. I accepted the award for her posthumously at the ASID convention. It acknowledged that all of these institutions had contributed to the development of Aspen as a cultural community and a center of intellectual thought where liberal democratic ideas flourish, humanitarian principles are practiced, and human rights are supported.

It was to this vibrant place that Judith and Edward Neisser migrated in the late 1980s after ten years in Vail. They bought one of the only condominiums in the historic West End. When I first walked its dusty streets nearly forty years before, it was a roughly eight-block-square area dotted with shabby clapboard-covered miners' cottages built by carpenters in the 1880s, probably from Victorian pattern books. In the ensuing years, these cottages have evolved into million-dollar homes that, amazingly, still maintain much of their original charm, even after extensive remodelings, thanks to the evolution of stringent zoning practices.

Judy and Ed returned to Aspen as often as Ed's business would allow, always inviting friends to share their three-bedroom condo and partake of the many pleasures of the mind as well as of the body for which the resort had become world-renowned. The first two summers after Ed's death, Judy's vigor was understandably at a low ebb, but gradually the restorative qualities of Aspen began to take effect. She started to write again and considered joining the writer's workshop there. Some of her friends connected with the Aspen Institute and the Aspen Art Museum

began to involve her in these cultural institutions. Judy decided her third summer to make a commitment to Aspen and build a house there. To do so she reassembled the Tigerman McCurry team, and it was my turn to produce the first plan.

We found an old house for sale on Francis Street near the corner of Fourth Street in the middle of the West End. It was undoubtedly a miner's cottage that had been so mutilated over the years that it was unidentifiable. Happily it did not qualify as a historic building that required restoration, and we were free to tear down this ugly duckling, which we did as soon as Judy closed on the property. Besides being a sunny lot that was not shaded in the late afternoon by Shadow Mountain, as was much of Aspen's business district, it had as its neighbor to the east an unusual home designed by Aspenite Harry Teague, the architect grandson of the great industrial designer Walter Dorwin Teague.

Before I drew a line for the ninety-by-one-hundred-foot lot, we ordered a new topographical survey that not only located all the trees with their respective calipers and species but also recorded the footprints of the adjoining neighbors. We contracted with a local architectural firm, Gibson Reno, to guide us through the intricacies of the Aspen building process from code compliance to contractor selection and to assist us in site supervision. Dave Gibson was a friend from the AIA Committee on Design, and Augie Reno was a graduate of the University of Illinois at Chicago during Stanley's tenure and a former Aspen city councilman.

The city of Aspen had instituted a number of building ordinances, one of which dealt with vegetation. There were certain sacred cows in the Aspen arboreal world, and one of these was the cottonwood tree—in spite of the fact that it is not a species indigenous to Aspen. We were resigned to preserving those

that were on the property, but there was a cluster of tall pines next to the existing house that actually prevented us from complying with other ordinances. One of them, aimed at maintaining a street presence, decreed that 60 percent of the facade of a new residence must be built within two feet of a line drawn between the fronts of the two neighboring residences, assuming that each is also located at the common ten-foot front-yard-setback line. To remove the pines, we needed to submit a tree-mitigation plan to the Parks Department that pointed out which trees would be taken out and also indicated how many new trees would be planted to ensure that the total number of caliper inches would remain the same. For example, if a twenty-four-inch-diameter tree is removed, it must be replaced by either eight three-inch-diameter trees or twelve two-inch-diameter trees. What has happened, of course, as this process continues, is

that the city is becoming engulfed in greenery.

The Planning and Zoning Commission had also established floor-area-ratios for various sized lots. Judy's nine-thousand-square-foot lot was one of the larger ones within the historic district and it actually qualified as a duplex. One ordinance had a number of other building restrictions and design standards that were developed with the help of the San Francisco architect Daniel Solomon to ensure that the scale and character of historic Aspen was always maintained. They were structured to promote designs that produced gable-roofed schemes with single-story porches that closely approximated the appearance of the nineteenth-century Victorians interspersed among them. Certain design guidelines dictated that a one-story, street-facing element must account for at least 20 percent of the total width of the building and that if an adjacent house or section thereof is one story,

then the new house needs to be one story for twelve feet across its front. Since Victorians are known for their twelve-in-twelve and greater roof pitches, the rules also stated that the steeper the roof pitch, the higher the roof can be raised. An architect is actually penalized for selecting a shallow pitch or a flat roof. There were numerous other restrictions, such as the requirement to separate first- and second-story windows by three feet to avoid large displays of glass. All of these rules I kept in mind as I organized the plan.

Judy, fortunately, was not a traditionalist. All of the historic houses in the neighborhood that were patterned after Eastern antecedents had steeply pitched, cross-gabled roofs with valleys and shallowly pitched porch roofs. Both of these configurations were the antithesis of what was appropriate for coping with the massive snowfalls that begin in the late fall and carry on through the spring. Many of the older houses wear heat

cables all winter or hire caretakers to shovel off the heaviest snow loads. Harry Teague's house for his brother had already broken the Victorian mold by introducing rusted corrugated metal, roofing paper, and primary-colored wood for siding, as well as multicolored steel windows. This ad hoc mix, although it adroitly used the prized gable roof, had more of an affinity with the industrial buildings the miners had erected near their claims on the mountain than with the Victorians in town.

The view to Aspen Mountain was from the rear of the house, and the first strategy was to organize the public rooms to take advantage of that view and the southern exposure that went with it. I started the plan in the northeast corner of the lot at the setback lines, having decided that if the twelve-foot-wide-by-sixteen-foot-deep master bedroom occupied that corner, it could satisfy the one-story-for-twelve-feet rule while simultaneously relating to the one-story Teague living room, which was also sixteen feet deep and canted off the north-west corner of its lot. Mindful of other rules, I stepped back the next three sections of ten feet, eight feet, and ten feet in increments of two feet, returning back to the lot line for the last twelve-foot section. Those moves satisfied the 60-percent rule and took full advantage of the sixty feet of footage allowed across the front that, combined with thirty feet of side-yard setbacks, totaled ninety feet.

I began the plans in the late fall without any preconception of what three-dimensional form the house

might assume stylistically but convinced that the stepped proportions would achieve the scalar reductions that would relate our design to those produced in the last century. Aspen is a city of mostly attractive alleys, and the powers that be prefer them to be used for vehicular access to one's house to maintain the illusion of a pre-automotive era. Therefore, the garage moved to the rear and with it went the mudroom/laundry that connected to the kitchen. That room, in turn, was to be a part of the main living/dining room to encourage informal gatherings. This public assemblage was stepped back

twenty-six feet to the west from Judy's bedroom suite so that those private rooms had direct access to a rear terrace, which at the time still contained the two remaining tall pines. Just off this terrace, Maria Smithburg, the landscape architect, planned a woodland pool with a bubbler to lull people to sleep. She also designed a secret garden that was enclosed by some of the many pines we had promised to plant in our tree-mitigation plan. Even though the kitchen became largely confined by adjacent rooms, it looked into what I envisioned as a very high-ceilinged great room that opened onto the terrace that extended all the way across the back room. Because the kitchen was set back against the ten-foot side yard, it was able to poke out into the front yard for seven feet, permitting a french door to open onto the front terrace. Three windows look out at a pole fence separating Judy's yard from her western neighbor, but Maria used up many more calipers planting a continuous row of aspens the length of this border. The trees were also intended to shade the house in summer from the strong western sun, as the garage shaded and screened the terrace.

The second floor contained the two additional guest suites that ostensibly completed Judy's program (the first-floor library doubling as a third). An L-shaped stair rose from the foyer to a bridge across it overlooking the entrance and connecting the two guest rooms, their baths disposed directly above other baths below. I thought at this point that the plan was set with the square footage well below Aspen's guidelines and the budget within reason—by local standards. Then our associate architects announced that, according to another new ordinance, Judy needed either to increase the budget by a number that when multiplied by the current square footage added approximately $50,000 to the project or to

add an affordable dwelling unit onto her house, deeding it to the city of Aspen to be rented only to an Aspenite. If she didn't add the unit, her $50,000 would be used to build affordable housing elsewhere for local employees. We chose to add another five hundred square feet to the project, tucking the extra unit above the kitchen and garage and accessing it from a stair opposite the laundry.

Stanley had been watching as I maneuvered my way through the maze of building restrictions, shaking his head at my stoic progress on the plans until it was time to manipulate the elevations. What form the house would take would be in large part a product of the roof lines. The house would sit some blocks from the base of Shadow Mountain, which shaded the lower portion of Aspen Mountain in the afternoon. In fact the city of Aspen is ringed by mountains, including Red Mountain on its north side. These mountains are never entirely benign, and some, like Stanley, find them downright menacing. The thin air, fickle winds, extremely heavy snowfalls, and deadly avalanches (often heralded by early morning Avalanche Control cannons) create an ever-present edge of danger that heightens one's awareness of the need for shelter. Stanley and I wanted Judith's home to signify shelter. We wanted it to be apparent that this was a structure made to survive the snow. Its staggered, stepped, steel roofs shed the snow that slides down them; snow guards are bolted to the edge of the eaves. When the snow piles up at the base of the house, it does so against an impervious red stone base. This is a house not unlike the mountains themselves in form. It is tied to the vernacular of the Victorians only by its small scale, its clapboard siding, and its double-hung windows. Otherwise it is, as best we can define it, an interpretation of the spirit of Aspen.

HARRIS HOUSE

Sawyer, Michigan
1996–98

Little did I know when I was an eight-year-old peering under the canvas flaps of the music tent in Aspen that Irving Harris was sitting inside along with my parents, listening to a seminar organized by the Aspen Institute. A young Chicagoan in his thirties, he too had learned of the interesting intellectual climate promulgated by the Paepckes in Aspen and had come to the mountains that first summer to partake of the institute's programs. Eighteen years later, in 1968, drawn by the Music Festival, Joan Frank paid her first visit to Aspen, arriving for a two-week vacation with her three children; they stayed six weeks. Although she and Irving became nodding acquaintances her first summer in Aspen, it was not until they met again in Chicago, as volunteers on Adlai Stevenson's political campaign, that their common interests in Democratic issues, music, and each other led to marriage.

As a consequence of their mutual appreciation of Aspen, the couple bought a house on North Street near the Aspen Meadows, the campus of the institute, and began to spend their summers there, arriving for the Aspen Design Conference in early June and leaving when the Music Festival figuratively folded its tent around Labor Day. They also spend time there in the winter. By the time the couple married, Irving had successfully founded several companies including the Harris Group, an investment-counseling firm that, after Irving sold it to his younger associates, changed its name to Harris Associates at about the time Edward Neisser joined them, further enriching the web of intricate social relationships.

After Judy and Ed relocated their vacation home to Aspen, and Stanley and I began to be frequent guests there, Judy always included a dinner with Irving and Joan as part of our visit. As long-time Aspenites, the Harrises developed many friendships with local professionals, including several artists and artisans who spent part of the summer conducting workshops at the Anderson Ranch, an arts center located on Owl Creek Road in Snowmass. But of all the cultural institutions with which the couple were involved, the Music Festival was Joan's major concern. Held in the old canvas tent for over forty years, concerts were subject to the vagaries of the weather and there was woefully inadequate rehearsal space. The board, of which Joan was a trustee, determined to build in the Meadows a permanent structure that would house a five-hundred-seat concert hall that would also be suitable for chamber music and have rehearsal and classroom space. The Harris Foundation provided the first major start-up gift, Joan ran the campaign to raise the rest of the money, and the Joan and Irving Harris Concert Hall, designed by Harry Teague, was dedicated in 1993. Their friend, Pussy Paepcke, in her ninetieth year, attended the opening-night ceremony.

Joan has also been involved in civic projects in Chicago, including the efforts to fund and/or build the Music and Dance Theater of Chicago and the Museum of Contemporary Art. A member of the architectural selection committee for both projects, she has worked with well-known architects and has developed her own sense of the aims of architectural endeavors, including a directness of expression in theoretical aspirations as well as in material usages.

Joan and Irving became my clients late in the summer of 1996, when they decided to build a weekend house in Harbor Country. This particular summer, the couple were confined to their condo in Chicago while Irving underwent eye surgery. Bereft of Aspen, Joan spent the summer commuting to Michigan, where her two sons and their families owned country cottages. When one daughter-in-law produced triplets, she and Irving realized that a family compound

within range of Chicago was not only desirable but almost necessary. Joan began to look for property in Berrien County. One day she called to say that an acquaintance was selling a twenty-three-acre parcel in Sawyer, near Wit's End. The property was several miles farther from the lake, but the Galien River ran through it, and Joan asked me to meet them there the next weekend to determine whether the house could be remodeled.

When I drove up the gravel drive it was to find, among tall pines, a rambling, semi-modern structure sitting on top of a ridge. The picture windows of the frame house overlooked an adjacent swimming pool and then several human-made ponds at the base of the ridge. The path from the house wound down the hill through an Italianate landscape with columnar cypresses arranged in rows and a stretch of lawn culminating in a small circular lily pond. Beyond this, a grassy land bridge spanned two of the ponds. The path then circumnavigated one pond and climbed up the hill again to terminate in an old apple orchard adjacent to the house on the ridge. It was an unusual, compelling landscape, and it reminded Joan of Connecticut, where she was raised. They decided to buy the property, even though Irving agreed that the existing house was neither designed nor constructed well enough to be a candidate for extensive remodeling. Instead it would become a guest house and we would build a new house farther along the ridge in the orchard, where it would overlook this same sylvan landscape. Joan and I immediately interviewed several landscape architects, selecting Maria Smithburg to prepare plans that would integrate the more manicured composition into an indigenous landscape of easily maintainable prairie grasses and native perennials.

Knowing that the house would stretch out along the ridge to take advantage of the landscape influenced its form. Since it was to be a house built around family interactions, we discussed the need for easy accessibility. A large informal two-story living-and-dining room with a

kitchen would be the core of activity. The great room would seat sixteen for dinner and at least eight for lounging around the fireplace or piano. The kitchen would have a table for six as well as a settee for gossiping with the cook or listening to the news on television. All the other accouterments of a well-stocked working kitchen would be part of the space, and ideally, from its windows, Joan would observe family comings and goings. The kitchen would also connect to the garage. Entrances to the house, whether through the front or rear doors, would be comfortably sized with spaces to assemble as well as to shed outdoor clothing and equipment with dispatch. The master suite

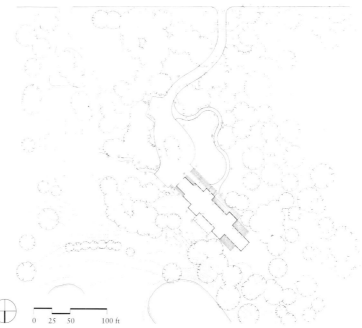

0   25   50   100 ft

would complete the ground floor. To accommodate guests, two generous bedrooms with accompanying baths would be located on the second floor along with an area for guests to congregate. Joan originally thought her office might be on this level as well, although Irving was to have one on the first floor. The house would be ringed by porches and decks.

I began the plan's progression along the ridge with the garage, which the couple agreed could be a single stall with room for equipment storage. The garage stepped outward in equal increments to allow for a pair of glazed access doors; these aligned with a second pair that opened on axis into a catchall room that was part pantry, part laundry, and part mudroom. It also had a stair that led to a large playroom in the basement. A third set of french doors, also on axis, opened into the kitchen on one side and the foyer on the other, two spaces that again step out incrementally. Both rooms then open onto the great room, completing two sets of axes. The great room shares the basilica plan of Boardwalk come full circle, the clerestory windows bringing light into the center of the room and tall transomed doors framing views to the terrace on the southwest and through the screened porch opposite to the pond and river beyond the trees.

The symmetrically dimensioned plan repeats itself as a mirror image on the opposite side of the room, as paired sliding french doors lead to the master bath, closets, and study. Two extra children's sleeping lofts perched above the closets are lit by the clerestory windows. New axes begin as two hallways open onto the master bedroom. This room completed the march along the ridge through the orchard, ending within twenty feet of the woods, until Joan decided to add an indoor exercise pool like the one they have in Aspen. And so a room for the "endless pool" attached itself to the master suite, its

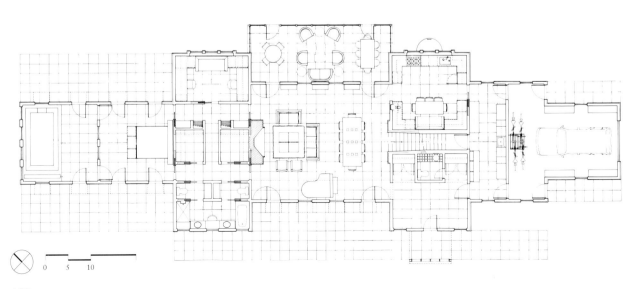

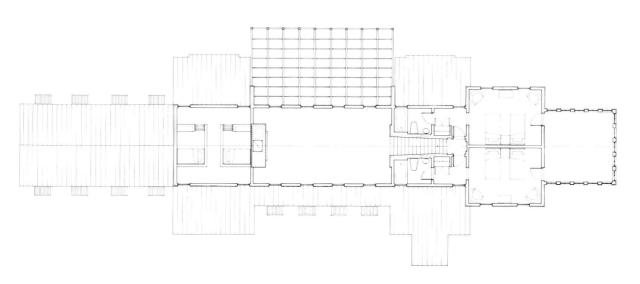

end windows almost touching a grove of fir trees on the periphery of the orchard.

Like a long corrugated-metal extrusion, the form is sheathed in industrial materials that are at once practical and reasonably economical. The vernacular of the region informs the series of stepped rectangles with their simple gable roofs that in the center section skip down to shed roofs. The galvanized metal siding slips down from the underside of the metal standing-seam roof. Corrugated-steel siding peels back above the doors to form protective canopies. The gabled ends of the buildings are clad in a concrete-tile grid that refer to Eastern antecedents. It also reminds one that this project is a human-made elemental building set down in the landscape like a solitary but serene object. It is not exactly one with nature, but it is not entirely opposed to it either. It is a redefinition and reassembly of familiar forms, each element recalling tradition without repeating it verbatim.

Once, Irving asked if I had ever designed a house with less intervention from the husband. He had agreed early on that this was to be Joan's project down to her selection of an old friend from New Haven, Sylvan Shemitz, as the lighting consultant. Joan and I expanded on the industrial aesthetic of the exterior in the interior detailing and materials. The furnishings are friendly to the extended family, including a series of four two-by-two-foot coffee tables, made by Lee Lyon, a glass artist in Aspen, that both reflect the grid and refer to the craft of glassmaking. The two-by-two grid of the radiant-heated limestone floors is repeated on a larger scale in the maple plywood panels bolted to the stair walls. All detailing is spare and purposeful in conception and realization, so that the structure has that sense of timelessness that Joan believes is one of the aims of all architectural endeavors.

PROJECT INFORMATION

Boardwalk
Lakeside, Michigan 1982–83
Design Partners: Margaret McCurry and Stanley Tigerman
Photographers: Jim Hedrich, Hedrich Blessing; Tony Soluri for *Architectural Digest*

Raymond Waites, Bettye Martin, and Norma Skurka. *American View*. New York: Harper & Row, 1984, 31, 206–7.

Michael Webb. *Architects House Themselves*. Washington: Preservation Press, 1984, 205–8.

Susan Doubilet. "A Piece of the American Quilt." *Progressive Architecture*, April 1984, 118–21.

Vincent Scully. "Architecture: Margaret McCurry Stanley Tigerman." *Architectural Digest*, April 1984, 156–63, 194–95.

N.R.G. "Sophisticated Use of Rural Vernacular." *Architecture*, May 1984, 204–6.

Susan S. Szenasy. *The Home: Exciting New Designs for Today's Lifestyles*. New York: MacMillan, 1985, cover, 46, 97, 126.

"Outdoor Rooms Go Post-Modern." *Metropolitan Home*, June 1985, 94.

"Corrugated Cottage." *Better Homes and Gardens*, fall 1986, 52–56.

Kathleen Quigley. "Their Kind of Town." *Town & Country*, September 1990, 283.

Monica Geran. "Tigerman McCurry." *Interior Design*, December 1990, 120–21.

"Tigerman McCurry." *Architectural Digest*, August 15, 1991, 232–33.

Anatxu Zabalbeascoa. *La Casa del Arquitecto*. Barcelona: Gustavo Gili, 1995, 146–49.

Susan Zevon. *Inside Architecture: Interiors by Architects*. Massachusetts: Rockport, 1996, 130–41.

Christine Pittel. "Architects at Home." *House Beautiful*, October 1996, 124.

Lisa Skolnik. "Pun House: Two Architects Play with the Concept of Boardwalk." *Chicago Tribune Magazine*, April 6, 1997, 34–39.

Stephen A. Kliment. "Tigerman McCurry." *Residential Architect*, July–August 1998, 54–55.

Awards: AIA National Honor Award for Excellence in Architectural Design, May 1984; AIA Chicago Chapter Distinguished Building Award, 1984; Builder's Choice Grand Award, Builders Magazine, 1985

Suhu Gallery
Chicago, Illinois, 1982–83
Design Partner: Margaret McCurry
Project Assistant: Joan Yanchewski
Photographer: Howard N. Kaplan, HNK Architectural Photography

Robert Bruegmann. "Little Journeys to the Offices of Architects." *Inland Architect*, May–June 1983, 9–11.

John G. Tucker. "For Art's Sake." *Interior Design*, December 1983, 178–81.

Robert Janjigian. "Rooms with a View." *Interiors*, January 1984, 172–73.

Madelyn Roesch and Cynthia Davidson-Powers. "A Walk on the Inside: Chicago Interiors." *Inland Architect*, January–February 1984, 20–21.

Monica Geran. "Tigerman McCurry." *Interior Design*, December 1990, 120–21.

Awards: AIA Chicago Chapter Interior Architecture Award Citation of Merit, 1983; *Interiors* Magazine Big I Award, 1983

Juvenile Protective Association
Chicago, Illinois, 1983–84
Design Partner: Margaret McCurry
Managing Partner: Robert Fugman
Project Assistant: Andrew Koglin
Photographer: Jon Miller, Hedrich Blessing

Awards: AIA Chicago Chapter Distinguished Building Award for Excellence in Architecture, 1986

Herman Miller
Chicago, Illinois, 1984–86
Design Partner: Margaret McCurry
Managing Partner: Robert Fugman
Project Assistant: Richard Dakich
Photographers: Barbara Karant, Karant & Associates; Nick Merrick, Hedrich Blessing

"Drama, Serenity, Primitivism: A Look at Herman Miller Showrooms." *Herman Miller Magazine*, 1985, 17–20.

Nora J. Rubinstein. "Margaret McCurry Collaborates with Herman Miller's Facilities Design Group to Design a New Showroom." *Interiors*, May 1985, 262–65.

Edie Lee Cohen. "The Merchandise Mart Showroom as Designed by Tigerman Fugman McCurry Architects." *Interior Design*, January 1986, 256–67.

Pilar Viladas. "Designing for Design." *Progressive Architecture*, February 1986, 106–9.

Awards: AIA Chicago Chapter Certificate of Merit, June 7, 1988; *Interiors* Magazine, AIA Chicago, Product Display Award, 1985

Wit's End: The Glass House
Sawyer, Michigan, 1985–87
Design Partner: Margaret McCurry
Project Assistant: John Holbert
Photographers: Bruce Van Inwegen, Van Inwegen Photography; Greg Murphy

"Single Family Housing." *Currents from Chicago: Recent Trends in Residential Architecture*, September–December 1986, 8.

Chicago Architectural Club Journal. New York: Rizzoli, 1987, 126.

Joseph Giovannini. "Vernacular Elements Shape a Rural Michigan Residence." *Architectural Digest*, April 1988, 52–56.

Judith Neisser. "Hot Houses: Stately Cottage." *Chicago City Living*, summer 1989, 19–23.

Wendy W. Staebler. *Architectural Detailing in Residential Interiors*. New York: Whitney Library of Design, 1990, 179.

Stephen A. Kliment. "Tigerman McCurry." *Residential Architect*, July–August 1998, 56–57.

Coulton Pond Ranch
Clark, Colorado, 1986–89
Design Partner: Margaret McCurry
Project Team: John Holbert, Karen Kramer Hollander, June Nelson-Steinke
Photographers: Robert Pisano for *Architectural Digest*; Tim Murphy for Alpine Log Homes

Suzanne Stephens. "In the Pioneer Spirit." *Architectural Digest*, June 1991, 152–53.

Suzanne Stephens. "Il richiamo della foresta." *AD Architectural Digest* (Italian edition), January 1992, 118–21.

Sally Stich. "Steamboat Symmetry." *Colorado Homes & Lifestyles*, May–June 1992, 30–37.

"Log Construction Renewed." *Architecture*, January 1993, 96–97.

Arthur Thiede and Cindy Teipner Thiede. *The Log Home Book*. Gribbs-Smith Publications, 1994.

Camp Madron
Madron Lake, Michigan, 1987
Design Partner: Margaret McCurry
Project Team: Karen Kramer Hollander, James T. Dallman

Haworth
Chicago, Illinois, 1988–90; 1992
Design Partner: Margaret McCurry
Project Team: Karen Lillard, Leslie Haines, David Knudson, Bruce Johnson, Chris Gryder, Tsi Ling Yap
Photographers: Abby Sadin and Ben Altman, Sadin Photo Group

Monica Geran. "Haworth, Chicago: To Introduce a New Product Selection, Margaret McCurry Designs a Showstopper." *Interior Design*, January 1989.

"Best of the WestWeek." *Contract*, August 1989, 94.

Monica Geran. "Midwest Industry Supplies the Theme Reinterpreted by Tigerman McCurry Architects." *Interior Design*, October 1990, 240–43.

Awards: *Interiors* Magazine, AIA Chicago, Product Display Award, Neo-Con 1988

Brandenburg Lake House
Fox Lake, Illinois, 1988–89
Design Partner: Margaret McCurry
Project Assistant: Roger Ferris
Renderings: Rene Stratton and Roger Farris

Hill Road House
Winnetka, Illinois, 1988–98
Design Partners: Margaret McCurry and Stanley Tigerman
Project Team: Richard Dragisic, Melany Telleen, Beverly J. Dahl, Chris Garvin, Karen Swanson, Laura Estes
Interior Design: John Mark Horton
Photographers: Steve Hall, Hedrich Blessing (interior); Bruce Van Inwegen, Van Inwegen Photography (exterior)

Chicago Bar Association
Chicago, Illinois, 1988–90
Design Partners: Margaret McCurry and Stanley Tigerman
Project Team: Paul Gates, Richard Dragisic, Julie Evans, Michael Pierry, Tom Leung, David Tsevat
Photographers: Bruce Van Inwegen, Van Inwegen Photography; Barbara Karant, Karant & Associates; Steve Hall, Hedrich Blessing

Heidi Landecker. "American Gothic." *Architecture*, June 1991, 72–75.

Timberlane House
New Buffalo, Michigan, 1989–90
Design Partner: Margaret McCurry
Project Team: Roger Ferris, David Knudson

Model: Roger Ferris
Model Photographer: Orlando Cabanban

University Club
Chicago, Illinois, 1989–91
Design Partner: Margaret McCurry
Project Team: Beverly J. Dahl, Tsi Ling Yap
Interior Design: John Mark Horton
Photographer: Jon Miller, Hedrich Blessing

Tom Finan. "Room with a View." *Club Management*, May 1992, 28, 31–39.

Awards: ASID Design Project Award, 1992; ASID First Place Interior Design Specialty Award, 1994

The Lighthouse
Martha's Vineyard, Massachusetts, 1991–93
Design Partner: Margaret McCurry
Project Team: Richard Nelson, Beverly J. Dahl
Landscape Architect: Michael R. Van Valkenburgh Associates, Inc.
Photographer: Richard Mandelkorn for *Architectural Digest*

Suzanne Stephens. "Nautical Illusions on Martha's Vineyard." *Architectural Digest*, June 1995, 190–97.

Justus House
Hinsdale, Illinois, 1992–93
Design Partner: Margaret McCurry
Project Assistant: Catherine Carr
Landscape Architect: Maria Smithburg, Artemisia
Photographer: Bruce Van Inwegen, Van Inwegen Photography

Stephen A. Kliment. "Tigerman McCurry." *Residential Architect*, July–August 1998, 58–61.

The Preserve
New Buffalo, Michigan, 1987–93
Design Partner: Margaret McCurry
Project Assistant: Dante Dommenella
Photographer: Bruce Van Inwegen, Van Inwegen Photography

Awards: AIA Chicago Chapter Distinguished Building Award Citation of Merit, 1994

Reinke Residence

New Buffalo, Michigan, 1993–95
Design Partner: Margaret McCurry
Project Team: Dante Dommenella, Susan O'Brien
Photographer: Bruce Van Inwegen, Van Inwegen Photography

John Riha. "Where Family Comes First." *Traditional Home*, March 1997, 77–89.

Nineteenth-Century Farmhouse

Rockford, Illinois, 1992–94
Design Partner: Margaret McCurry
Project Team: Melany Telleen, Susan O'Brien
Photographer: Tony Soluri, Soluri Photography for *Architectural Digest*

Judith Neisser. "Rethinking a 19th Century Illinois Farmhouse." *Architectural Digest*, February 1996, 42–56, 50.

Prairie Crossing

Grayslake, Illinois, 1992–99
Design Partner: Margaret McCurry
Project Team: Mark Lehman, Christopher Nigro, Stephanie Anuszkiewicz, Ted Buenz, Susan O'Brien, Dong Huy Kim
Photographer: Bruce Van Inwegen, Van Inwegen Photography

Seka Prodanovic. "Old is New." *Chicago Tribune*, April 22, 1995, section 4, 3.

Frank Edgerton Martin. "Riverside Revisited?" *Landscape Architecture*, August 1995.

Wendy Talarico. "The Nature of Green Architecture." *Architectural Record*, April 1998, 149–52.

Nancy D. Holt. "How 'Green' is Your Household?" *Wall Street Journal*, May 22, 1998, Home Front.

William Weathersby Jr. "Houses as Products: Prairie Crossing, Grayslake, Illinois." *Architectural Record*, January 1999, 120–23.

Michigan Shores Club

Wilmette, Illinois, 1992–99
Design Partner: Margaret McCurry
Project Team: Melany Telleen, Rocco Castellano, Susan O'Brien, Dante Dommenella, Chris Garvin
Photographer: Bruce Van Inwegen, Van Inwegen Photography

Wildwood

Bridgman, Michigan, 1993–94
Design Partner: Margaret McCurry
Project Team: David Armitage, Susan O'Brien
Landscaper: Gunner Pioter, Riveria Gardens
Photographers: Jim Hedrich, Hedrich Blessing; Bruce Van Inwegen for *Architectural Digest*

Joseph Giovannini. "Midwestern Farmhouse with a Modern Soul." *Architectural Digest*, June 1996, cover, 104–11, 200.

"Calendar." *Residential Architect*, October 1998.

McClintock Camp

Grand Marais, Michigan, 1994–96
Design Partner: Margaret McCurry
Project Assistant: Susan O'Brien
Photographer: Christopher Barrett, Hedrich Blessing

Kevin M. Williams. "Exhibit Offers Architect's-Eye View." *Chicago Sun-Times*, January 15, 1999, arts section, NC 49.

Exhibitions: "Women in Architecture," Department of Architecture at the Art Institute of Chicago, Gallery 24, 1998

Neisser Condominium

Chicago, Illinois, 1994–96
Design Partners: Margaret McCurry and Stanley Tigerman
Project Assistants: Stephanie Anuszkiewicz, Melany Telleen, Dong Huy Kim
Lighting Design: Sylvan R. Shemitz Associates, Inc.
Photographers: Steve Hall, Hedrich Blessing; Timothy Hursley for *Architectural Digest*

Paul Goldberger. "Modern Classicism for Chicago." *Architectural Digest*, April 1997, 167–75, 219.

Judith P. Knuth. "Two Homes Garner Awards for 'Controlled Simplicity.'" *Focus*, November 1997, 21–22.

"1998 Honor Awards." *AIArchitect*, February 1998, 12.

"Honor Awards Interiors." *Architectural Record*, May 1998, 119.

Awards: AIA National Honor Award for Interior Architecture, 1998; AIA Chicago Chapter Interior Architecture Honor Award, 1997

Neisser House

Aspen, Colorado, 1995–97
Design Partners: Margaret McCurry and Stanley Tigerman
Site Architects: Gibson Reno Architects
Project Team: Stephanie Anuszkiewicz, Jenny Han, Melany Telleen
Landscape Architect: Maria Smithburg, Artemisia
Lighting Design: Sylvan R. Shemitz Associates, Inc.
Photographers: Steve Hall, Hedrich Blessing; Mary Nichols for *Architectural Digest*

Mildred Schmertz. "Architecture: Mining the Aspen Vernacular." *Architectural Digest*, May 1999, 214–21, 237.

Harris House

Sawyer, Michigan, 1996–98
Design Partner: Margaret McCurry
Project Team: Ben Loomis, Chris Davis, Jeff Phelps, Kevin Stephenson
Landscape Architect: Maria Smithburg, Artemisia
Lighting Design: Sylvan R. Shemitz Associates, Inc.
Photographer: Steve Hall, Hedrich Blessing

Awards: AIA Chicago Chapter Distinguished Building Award, 1999

Exhibitions: "At Home in Chicago, Part I," Department of Architecture at the Art Institute of Chicago, Gallery 24, 1999

BIOGRAPHY

Margaret I. McCurry, FAIA IIDA ASID, is a principal in the architectural firm Tigerman McCurry. The firm's practice includes cultural, institutional, and commercial buildings, as well as residential projects throughout the United States. In addition, McCurry has designed furnishings, fabrics, and accessories.

McCurry received her bachelor's degree in art history from Vassar College in 1964 and spent two semesters as a Loeb Fellow at the Harvard Graduate School of Design in 1986–87, where she is currently president of the Alumni/ae Council. She has received several Honor Awards from the American Institute of Architects, numerous Distinguished Building and Interior Architecture Awards from the Chicago chapter of the AIA, and both national and local Interior Design Project Awards from the American Society of Interior Designers. In 1990 she was inducted into the Interior Design Hall of Fame.

Her work has been published widely in architectural and interiors magazines and exhibited at museums and galleries nationally and internationally; it is also in the permanent collections of the Department of Architecture at the Art Institute of Chicago and the Deutsches Architektur Museum in Frankfurt, Germany. McCurry has lectured at many architectural conferences and universities, and she has taught design studios at the School of the Art Institute of Chicago and the University of Illinois at Chicago.

In 1993 McCurry was chair of the national AIA Committee on Design. She was the vice president of the Chicago chapter of the AIA in 1987–89 and of the Architecture and Design Society of the Art Institute of Chicago, where she is currently a board member of the Textile Society. She regularly juries AIA awards programs and has been chair of the National Interior Architecture Awards jury. In addition, she has been a jury adviser for the National Endowment for the Arts. Since 1995 McCurry has held an appointment to the Public Buildings Service National Register of Peer Professionals of the U.S. General Services Administration.

ACKNOWLEDGMENTS

At the end of the introduction to this book I wrote, "The projects included here testify to my belief that taking one's own road, rather than racing around another's, is in the end the most satisfying and steady course." And so I dedicate this book to those who helped me along the way, to the memory of Paul D. McCurry and to Irene B. McCurry, two unique aesthetes who set me on my course. And also to my special mentor and spouse, Stanley Tigerman, who ootzes me onward if my steps ever lag and who patiently (most of the time) listened as I read and reread the chapters from this book, dishing out criticism and praise in equal measure. He has always encouraged the emergence of my voice, whether or not he agreed with what I was saying.

The practice of architecture, unlike the other fine arts, is rarely a solitary performance. Our clients share center stage; I must also acknowledge the supporting cast who assisted me in interpreting the clients' scripts, concretizing their programs, and constructing dwellings in which the dramas of ordinary lives may be played out in memorable settings. The clients whose stories are enacted here, anonymously or not, occupy the limelight.

It should also be shared by friends who read excerpts from the manuscript and volunteered advice, by those in our office who prepared the drawings and typed endless permutations of the text, by the editors who made sense of it all, by the graphic designer who sensitively constructed it, and by the publisher who initiated it. Thank you to all.

191

PHOTOGRAPHY AND RENDERING CREDITS